Russian Theater and Costume Designs

from The Fine Arts Museums of San Francisco

Introduction by John E. Bowlt

Catalogue prepared by Nikita D. Lobanov, Nina Lobanov, and Aimée Troyen

This catalogue was funded by The Museum Society
and published on the occasion of an exhibition at
The Fine Arts Museums of San Francisco,
January 19 – March 9, 1980.

Circulated by The Fine Arts Museums of San Francisco,
1980–82.

Copyright © 1979 by The Fine Arts Museums of San Francisco.
Printed in the United States of America.
All rights reserved.
ISBN 0-88401-033-3
Library of Congress Catalog Card No. 79-55788

Typeset by Custom Typography Service, San Francisco.
Printed by Cal-Central Press, Sacramento.
Color photography by James Medley.
Designed in San Francisco by Polly Bryson.

Cover: Léon Bakst, *Costume for Potiphar's Wife,*
La Légende de Joseph, 1914 (Cat. 11)

Contents

4 Preface

5 History of the Collection

12 Introduction

    The Catalogue

17 Frequently Cited References
17 Notes to the Catalogue

18 Boris Anisfeldt
18 Léon Bakst
25 Alexandre Benois
35 Eugène Berman
36 Boris Bilinsky
38 Dmitri Bouchène
42 Mstislav Doboujinsky
45 Alexandra Exter
45 Michel Georges-Michel
46 Alexandre Golovine
47 Natalia Gontcharova
50 Alexandre Jacovleff
51 Alexis Korovine
52 Mikhail Larionov
53 Marie Laurencin
54 Simon Lissim
55 Pablo Picasso
55 Pedro Pruna
56 José-Maria Sert
56 Sergei Soudeikine
60 Sergei Tchehonine
61 Pavel Tchelitchew

62 Bibliography

Preface

The year 1979 marks the fiftieth anniversary of the death of Sergei Diaghilev, the impresario who was the dynamic force behind the revolutionary Ballets Russes in the first decades of this century. It is fitting that the publication of *Russian Theater and Costume Designs from The Fine Arts Museums of San Francisco* honors this great innovator. At the same time it pays tribute to the memory of Mrs. Alma de Bretteville Spreckels, one of the founders of the California Palace of the Legion of Honor and a collector of considerable foresight. Her love for the dance inspired her to acquire many of the masterworks of Léon Bakst, Mikhail Larionov and Natalia Gontcharova at a time when most collectors overlooked the importance of their art. This catalogue is a testimony to her collecting instincts and continues the important responsibility of publishing the Museums' holdings.

The idea for this catalogue began in 1976 with the highly successful exhibition of many of these designs at The Society of Four Arts in Palm Beach. The arrival in San Francisco in 1976 of Nikita and Nina Lobanov served as a further catalyst. In addition to their research on the existing collection, which brought a new awareness of its importance, they gave to the Museums forty designs from their own distinguished collection. Their generosity cannot be overstated; without their efforts this catalogue would not have been possible.

Many individuals helped in innumerable ways in the preparation of this project. Particularly, I would like to thank Earl Anderson, Niccolo Caldararo, Mrs. Parmenia Ekstrom, Cheryl Faus, Robert Futernick, Thomas Carr Howe, James Medley, Martin Müller, Alden Murray, Brenda M. Palley, Ann Preece, Maxine Rosston, George Sexton, Nancy Van Norman-Baer, and the staff of the Archives of the Performing Arts, San Francisco Public Library. The enthusiastic support of the Director of Museums, Ian McKibbin White, and the Chairman of the Museum Society, John Lowell Jones, has been essential to this project and is gratefully acknowledged here.

It is a privilege to thank John E. Bowlt for his comprehensive and informative introduction. As a result of his research, we now have a deeper understanding and appreciation of the works in the collection.

The task of making this publication a reality became the responsibility of four individuals who accomplished their parts with great professionalism. Gail Larrick ably fulfilled her role as editor; Polly Bryson used flair and imagination in executing the design of the catalogue; and Ann Karlstrom, Publications Manager for the Museums, used considerable patience and talent in supervising the project through its various stages to completion. Finally, a special word of thanks goes to Aimée Troyen, Assistant Curator, for coordinating the catalogue and the subsequent exhibitions of this material. She has taken on this task outside her field of specialization and performed admirably.

Robert Flynn Johnson
Curator in Charge
Achenbach Foundation for Graphic Arts
Department of Prints and Drawings

History of the Collection

The refined taste and generous patronage of Mrs. Alma de Bretteville Spreckels (1881–1968) has frequently been acknowledged in the publications of The Fine Arts Museums of San Francisco. An eminent collector and a devotee of the arts, Mrs. Spreckels, along with her husband, Adolph B. Spreckels (1857–1924), founded the California Palace of the Legion of Honor in 1924. Throughout her life she continued to enrich the collections of the museum, which today is part of The Fine Arts Museums of San Francisco. Among other gifts was an important group of Rodin's sculptures, published by the Museums in 1977.[1]

One aspect of Mrs. Spreckels's generosity has until now been given less attention than is due: the gift of the exceptional collection of Russian theater and costume designs that she formed in the late 1950s. In 1977 this gift was joined by that of Mr. and Mrs. Nikita D. Lobanov,[2] prominent private collectors who resided in San Francisco from 1976 until mid-1979. Combined, these gifts represent one of the foremost collections of twentieth-century stage designs in the country today.

Mrs. Spreckels's interest in the history of theater and dance was not limited to Russian material. Her collection, which she started in the early years of the twentieth century, was initially inspired by her friend, the American dancer Loïe Fuller. Among Mrs. Spreckels's first purchases were posters, drawings, and sculptures of Loïe as well as of Isadora Duncan. In the late 1940s she acquired a number a bronzes of famous dancers by Malvina Hoffman, whom she had met when the sculptress was studying in Rodin's studio.

During one of her frequent trips to Europe in the mid-1950s, Mrs. Spreckels met Constantin Joanidu, a Rumanian who lived in Paris. Joanidu was a ballet and opera enthusiast whose friendship with Boris Kochno and Serge Lifar gave him access to important European collections of Russian stage designs. Since Mrs. Spreckels was interested in acquiring works from the Diaghilev era, she hired Joanidu as her consultant.

After her return to San Francisco, Mrs. Spreckels and Joanidu corresponded frequently.[3] He wrote her lengthy descriptions of the pieces he had found and occasionally sent photographs. Thomas Carr Howe, then the Director of the California Palace of the Legion of Honor, advised Mrs. Spreckels on her purchases. In June 1958 he met Joanidu in Paris and accompanied him to the studio of Boris Kochno. Together, they were instrumental in persuading Kochno to part with some of the treasures in his possession. Joanidu made his first purchases for Mrs. Spreckels in January 1958; by the end of the year over fifty designs by Léon Bakst, Alexandre Benois, Mstislav Doboujinsky, Natalia Gontcharova and Mikhail Larionov had entered her collection.

Joanidu worked for Mrs. Spreckels until the beginning of 1959, at which time she ceased making purchases. She concentrated instead on plans to build a Museum of the Dance and Theater where her collection, which had been stored in the basement apartments of her mansion on Washington Street, could be permanently installed. Several proposals were made, including one for the construction of a pavilion opposite the main entrance to the California Palace of the Legion of Honor; a tunnel was to link the two buildings. These plans, however, were never realized. As the works in Mrs. Spreckels's collection became too numerous to be kept in her house, they were moved to the Legion. In the late 1950s they were exhibited as an extended loan in two of the upstairs galleries. Having put aside the idea of building a separate museum, Mrs. Spreckels gave her collection to the Legion in two large gifts — one in 1959, the other 1962. When the California Palace of the Legion of Honor and the M. H. de Young Memorial Museum were merged under one administration in 1972, the collection became part of The Fine Arts Museums of San Francisco.

In 1977 Mr. and Mrs. Nikita D. Lobanov presented forty costume and set designs to the Museums. Their gift was intended to augment the Spreckels collection — rich in material from the Diaghilev era — with representative works by the second generation of Russian stage designers. It included watercolors and drawings by Eugène Berman, Alexis Korovine, Sergei Soudeikine, Sergei Tchehonine and Pavel Tchelitchew.

Nikita Lobanov's interest in the ballet and the opera began when he was a child growing up in Bulgaria. Just after his arrival in Western Europe in 1954, he attended *The Diaghilev Exhibition* in London.[4] Intrigued by what he saw there, he became determined to start a collection of his own. But Lobanov was only eighteen at the time, an impoverished student at Oxford. During the next four years he sought out people who had witnessed the spectacles of the Ballets Russes. He also befriended the sisters of Boris Pasternak (1890–1960) and was introduced to the work of their father, Leonid Pasternak (1862–1945), a well-known Russian impressionist painter.

After finishing Oxford in 1958, Nikita moved to New York. There he met people who had worked with Diaghilev and began writing articles on the history of the Russian stage. In 1962 he and his wife, Nina, started collecting on a modest scale. Among their inital purchases were designs for two different productions of *Petrouchka*: those by Soudeikine for the production at the Metropolitan Opera House in 1925 and those by Benois for the production at La Scala in 1947.

Today the Lobanovs' collection consists of over seven hundred pieces. The eighty artists represented can be divided into three groups: Russian-born artists whom Diaghilev employed for his Ballets Russes, designers who worked for the offshoots of Diaghilev's company, and

Russian avant-garde artists who worked for the stage in Russia and western Europe. During the past fifteen years, parts of the collection have traveled throughout the country in exhibitions organized by the International Exhibitions Foundation, the University of Texas at Austin and other groups. In addition to their gift to The Fine Arts Museums of San Francisco, the Lobanovs have contributed theater and dance designs to The New York Public Library, The Metropolitan Museum of Art, New York, and the Museum of Modern Art, New York.

The Lobanov gift and the rising interest in the history of theater and dance brought to the Museums' attention the necessity of cataloguing their collection. This publication joins those of the Wadsworth Atheneum, Hartford, and The New York Public Library as a partial record of the extensive holdings of theater and dance designs in the United States today. It is hoped that this catalogue, in which many works are reproduced for the first time, will stimulate new research and encourage the documentation of other public and private collections.

The people of San Francisco, with their great love for the opera and the ballet, are privileged to have this wealth of material in their Museums. And in such an environment, this collection, whose foundations were so generously laid by Mrs. Alma de Bretteville Spreckels and Mr. and Mrs. Nikita D. Lobanov, should continue to give pleasure and to grow.

Aimée Troyen
Assistant Curator
Achenbach Foundation for Graphic Arts
Department of Prints and Drawings

Notes

1. Jacques de Caso and Patricia B. Sanders, *Rodin's Sculpture*, The Fine Arts Museums of San Francisco, 1977.
2. Their collection is usually referred to as the Lobanov-Rostovsky Collection.
3. Mr. Joanidu's letters to Mrs. Spreckels are in the library of the Department of Prints and Drawings (Achenbach Foundation for Graphic Arts), The Fine Arts Museums of San Francisco.
4. The *Diaghilev Exhibition,* organized by Richard Buckle, opened at the Edinburgh Festival on August 22, 1954 and was subsequently shown at Forbes House, London, November 3, 1954 to January 16, 1955.

Alexis Korovine
Backdrop, Act IV, Scene II,
The Invisible City of Kitezh, 1929 (Cat. 72)

Natalia Gontcharova
Project for Decor, Act I,
Le Coq d'Or, 1914 (Cat. 62)

Léon Bakst
Costume for an Old Jew Holding the Head of Holofernes,
Judith, 1922 (Cat. 14)

Léon Bakst
Costume for a Jewish Dancer and a Black Slave,
1921 (Cat. 13)

Alexandre Golovine
Decor,
Orphée, 1926 (Cat. 61)

Introduction

During the past decade more than fifteen exhibitions of material related to Sergei Diaghilev (1872–1929) and the Ballets Russes have been held in European and American museums.[1] One might logically assume that the magic of Diaghilev and his dancers and designers would have begun to pall after such public exposure. On the contrary, the more closely we acquaint ourselves with the entire endeavor of early twentieth-century stage design, the more we appreciate its originality, its richness, its potential. Many artists were involved in productions by Diaghilev as well as those by other patrons such as Ida Rubinstein, Maria Kousnetsov and Colonel Wassily de Basil. The visual material preserved is quite extensive. Even so, the theatrical holdings of The Fine Arts Museums of San Francisco, dependent upon the donations of Mrs. Alma de Bretteville Spreckels and Mr. and Mrs. Nikita D. Lobanov, are exceptional. They represent the foremost artists of the golden age of stage decor and contain masterpieces of set and costume design — from Léon Bakst's *Hélène de Sparte* (Cat. 6) to Natalia Gontcharova's *Le Coq d'Or* (Cat. 62), from Alexandre Benois's *Le Pavillon d'Armide* (Cats. 16, 17) to Marie Laurencin's *Les Biches* (Cat. 76).

It is gratifying to realize that exciting discoveries can still be made in this area and that we now have a few more components of an intricate mosaic. With well over one hundred pieces, The Fine Arts Museums of San Francisco can be considered a major United States depository of twentieth-century stage design, along with The Museum of Modern Art, New York; The New York Public Library; the Stravinsky-Diaghilev Foundation, New York; the Wadsworth Atheneum, Hartford; and the private collections of Mr. and Mrs. Nikita D. Lobanov, Robert Tobin and the late Donald Oenslager.[2]

The collection of The Fine Arts Museums helps to fill certain gaps in our general knowledge of the Ballets Russes and other troupes and at the same time poses a number of questions. It focuses attention on little-known productions such as *Orphée* of 1926 (designed by Alexandre Golovine and Bakst) and the unrealized *Chota Roustaveli* of 1946 (designed by Gontcharova) and raises the issue of versions, variants, imitations and copies. For example, we find yet another repetition of Benois's backdrop for Armide's garden in Scene II of *Le Pavillon d'Armide* (Cat. 16) and a third or fourth ballerina for *Petrouchka* (Cat. 19);[3] we are also presented with a variant of Bakst's decor for Acts I and III of *Hélène de Sparte* (Cat. 6) and a variant of Mstislav Doboujinsky's decor for *Les Papillons* (Cat. 54).[4] This important issue connects with another aspect of the collection: designs made by Russian, European and American artists after the termination of Diaghilev's Ballets Russes in 1929. Inasmuch as the collection contains designs by Eugène Berman, Dmitri Bouchène and other members of the second generation of modern Russian stage designers, mention should be made of their status and role. First, however, let us recall some general historical facts about the development of the Russian stage, since the works of the Russian artists constitute the largest and most impressive contingent of The Fine Arts Museums' collection.

The Late Nineteenth Century

With the dominance of Realism during the late nineteenth century, the "theatricality" of the theater, present during the Baroque and Rococo epochs, was almost lost. The theater was no longer a realm of enchanting prefabrication but, instead, tended to focus on the sociopolitical issues of everday life. The Russian stage of this period did, however, avoid some of the excesses of the European stage; it was still young, having become a professional, sophisticated medium of expression only in the late eighteenth century — thanks to the cultural preferences and patronage of Catherine the Great. Although it retained a freshness and diversity, the Russian theater of the late nineteenth century was nonetheless affected by the negative tendencies of Victorian taste. The eclectic mixing of styles regardless of artistic or historical relevance was one such pernicious trend; another was the primary position of the virtuoso on the stage from the 1860s to the 1880s, a condition that undermined the artistic totality of the theater. Rather than an aesthetic environment deriving concurrently from the various arts, the actor, dancer or singer became the theater. Even with the experimental productions of Konstantin Stanislavsky at his Moscow Arts Theater from 1898 onwards, and the new dramas of Anton Chekhov, the actor still tended to be at the center of attention, the decor serving merely to amplify his or her gestures and speech. Stanislavsky, for all his great talents, still regarded stage design as description and, therefore, as a static medium.

Nevertheless, at the turn of the century some Russian producers and designers began to reject Stanislavsky's attitude and to move away from surface decoration in favor of a more spatial, architectonic orientation. This development coincided with the advent of the impresario who, by his or her very function, acted as an artistic integrator or synthesizer. The evolution of the modern Russian stage would have been unthinkable without the efforts of people such as Nikita Balieff, Diaghilev, Nikolai Evreinov, Jascha Juschny, Savva Mamontov, Vsevolod Meierkhold, Ida Rubinstein and Alexandr Tairov; they rearranged the elements of the theater and forced the concept of design to advance from its static, nineteenth-century role to its dynamic, twentieth-century one. Determined to imbue each production with a "certain plastic rhythm peculiar just to that particular performance,"[5] they invited artists rather than ethnographers into the theater and insisted that the designs participate in the action of the stage. In a word, they conceived the theater as theater, not as the handmaiden to literature and music.

In undertaking the commissions of these impresarios, Russian artists employed many styles and disciplines: from the rococo paraphrases of Alexandre Benois to the elegant Constructivism of Alexandra Exter, from the buffoonery of Gontcharova and Mikhail Larionov to the Art Deco of Boris Bilinsky, from the Jugendstil of Golovine to the Surrealism of Pavel Tchelitchew. Moreover, they did not confine themselves to the professional stage but also, in some cases, worked for the circus, the cabaret, the puppet theater and the cinema, although the ballet remained their primary medium.

The World of Art Group

Benois and Diaghilev were leaders of the society of artists, literati and aesthetes known as the World of Art *(Mir iskusstva)*, active in St. Petersburg in the late 1890s and the 1900s. Although the World of Art did not compile a systematic credo of art, it set as one of its aims the refurbishing of the Russian decorative arts. Consequently, most members of the World of Art, such as Bakst, Benois, Doboujinsky and Golovine, turned their attention to stage design, playing an important role in the international reputation of Diaghilev's Ballets Russes between 1909 and 1929. Discussion of the principles of stage design supported by Benois and Bakst helps to elucidate the reasons for their successful contribution to the history of modern Russian art and, in turn, to the strength and diversity of twentieth-century stage design as a whole.

Alexandre Benois

In the spring of 1907 the young dancer and choreographer Michel Fokine, who was teaching at the Theater School attached to the Imperial Ballet in St. Petersburg, invited Benois to design sets and costumes for a ballet he was choreographing — *Le Pavillon d'Armide*. The period of the ballet, the Regia Versaliarum, was to Benois's taste, and he accepted the commission — his first professional stage engagement — immediately. As he later recalled: "Each new idea demanded a discussion with [Nicholas] Tcherepnin and Fokine .... These discussions and collaborations belong to the most cherished memories of my life ...."[6]

In his designs for *Le Pavillon d'Armide,* Benois's remarkable gift for comprehending an historical epoch in all its details was evident. His talent was particularly apparent in his famous set for Scene II and the many costumes for the *dramatis personae* such as the Old Marquis and Armide herself. Still, in his endeavor to convey the spirit of a given historical period, Benois was sometimes guilty of pedantic compilation, especially in later life. Fortunately, this problem did not flaw *Le Pavillon d'Armide* or several ballets and operas that he decorated at home and abroad at this time, such as *Les Sylphides* (1909), *Giselle* (1910) and *Petrouchka* (1911). His design for *Giselle,* for instance, was so well received at its Paris premiere that it was repeated many times in its original format.

The climax of Benois's career was his design for the Diaghilev production of *Petrouchka* in Paris in 1911. Curiously, the artist — who by that time was a suave, middle-aged man commuting between St. Petersburg, Rome and Paris, and a sober, encyclopaedic scholar — scored a remarkable success with this seemingly "vulgar" and "childish" ballet. But *Petrouchka* was dear to Benois, and in creating its sets and costumes, he seemed to evoke fond memories of a childhood when the fairs, the Punch and Judy shows and the conjurors were still part of the low culture of St. Petersburg.

Benois returned to *Petrouchka* in several subsequent productions. Whether each drawing signed and dated 1911 was actually executed in that year is not always clear. The costumes in the collection of The Fine Arts Museums, for example, differ somewhat from their counterparts in the Russian Museum, Leningrad, and the Wadsworth Atheneum, which, beyond doubt, are original designs. They may relate to a later presentation, in spite of their inscriptions.

Benois collaborated with Stravinsky on other spectacles such as *Le Rossignol* of 1914, but none were possessed with the spontaneity and the sincerity of *Petrouchka*. Despite its dissonance and unconventionality, *Petrouchka* was a narrative ballet, and Benois, a traditionalist at heart, used sets and costumes as literary means of expression. Bakst, on the other hand, was a more original artist and questioned this procedure.

Léon Bakst

Bakst made his debut as a professional designer in February, 1902, with the St. Petersburg production of *Le Coeur de la Marquise,* a pantomime on which he had begun work in 1900. The production, which was performed only twice, is represented in The Fine Arts Museums by three designs, a component unparalleled in other European and American collections. These early works express a lyrical, "Wertherian" mood — the young man's hair ruffled in the wind, the bottle-green suit, the modest dress of Mlle. Baletta. Such ingenuous romanticism served as a precedent for Bakst's treatment of later ballets and operas set in the early nineteenth century.

Although *Le Coeur de la Marquise* evoked an historical time dear to many of the World of Art artists, it was not the only theme or period that fascinated Bakst. Ancient Greece and the Orient were his main historical and philosophical interests, as evidenced in a series of productions he designed beginning in 1902: *Hyppolytus*

(1902, 1904), *Oedipus Rex* (1904), *Antigone* (1904), *Narcisse* (1911), *Hélène de Sparte* (1912), and *Daphnis et Chloë* (1912). *Hyppolytus* and *Oedipus Rex* served both thematically and formally as prototypes for the later presentations. In them, Bakst's conception of Greece was already at odds with that traditionally held in the nineteenth century, and his costumes were unprecedented in their emphasis on rhythmic body movement. Ida Rubinstein was the first to appreciate these innovations, as she indicated in an article of 1913: "... I made my debut in St. Petersburg in the role of Antigone.... What a brilliant idea it was to ask Bakst to design my costume!... He endowed the human silhouette with the acuity and tragic sense that you feel when you read the classics. I made an artistic alliance with him, one of great value to me."[7] This alliance resulted in many important productions, including *Hélène de Sparte, La Pisanella* (1913) and *Orphée* (1926).

Bakst's visual conception of *Hélène de Sparte* was much indebted to his tour of Greece with Valentin Serov in 1907. He wrote of that journey, "What a lot of new impressions. They are so unexpected that all my previous, Petersburgian ideas of the heroic Hellas have been thrown into a clumsy pile. I now have to alter my thinking, order and 'classify' everything anew."[8] What he saw as the real Greece was not a civilization of elegant marble columns, of intellectual discipline and poise, but a highly emotional, archaic, heathen society. This interpretation bewildered the audience of *Hélène de Sparte,* accustomed to a nobler conception.[9] When we examine the set for Acts I and III with its primordial landscape, its carved figures and sacrificial fires, we are reminded more of the barbaric Russia of Nikolai Roerich's *Polovtsian Dances* than of classical Athens. This particular set was a centerpiece in Bakst's iconography, deriving from earlier landscapes (for example, from the main set in *Hyppolytus* and the *panneau* called *Terror Antiquus* of 1908) and anticipating other ballet designs such as the decor for *Daphnis et Chloë* and even for *Le Dieu Bleu* of the same year.

Bakst's ability to adjust certain fundamental design structures to various productions did not denote a lack of originality. Rather, it indicated how pressing were the constant demands on the artist's time and energy. In 1912 and '13, for example, Bakst designed no fewer than fifteen ballets. Undoubtedly, this pressure contributed to his illness and premature death. The question of Bakst's variations and variability is complicated; some images recur frequently in his pictorial and theatrical work. For example, Bakst's costume for Judith in the 1922 production of *Judith* is a modification of his costume for Karsavina of 1907 and for Rubinstein in *La Tragédie de Salomé* of 1913. The luxurious gown for Potiphar's Wife in *La Légende de Joseph* of 1914, which exists in at least nine versions,[10] became the prototype for a whole gallery of *femmes fatales* in spectacles such as the *Femmes de Bonne Humeur* (1918) and *The Sleeping Princess* (1921). This sumptuous heroine — who graced the frontispiece of the souvenir program for the production at the Theatre Royal, Drury Lane — blended perfectly with José-Maria Sert's splendid set (Cat. 81).

Bakst considered the human body to be a kinetic generator, a rhythmic force that was to be supplemented and amplified in its motion, not enveloped and arrested. He tried to make the *plastique* of the body as expressive as the music, the scenery or the plot by supplementing the physical movements of the body. He attached appendages — feathers, scarves and jewelry — to extend the movements into space, or created intricate, abstract patterns of dress that emphasized the body's passage through space.

Bakst did not expose the body merely for erotic appeal, although he did free it from its conventional role on stage. He did not sympathize with the vogue for nudity on stage that was evident in certain Russian circles during the 1910s and 1920s. Bakst delighted in the human form, but he saw its beauty in the tension between seen and unseen.

Mstislav Doboujinsky and Alexandre Golovine
Few of Bakst's colleagues were as responsive as he to new concepts of stage design. Their sets and costumes are, however, worthy of critical attention, for, on many occasions, they functioned well, even brilliantly. Doboujinsky's work, for example, typified the elegant restraint of the World of Art. His decorations for Ivan Turgenev's *A Month in the Country,* produced by Stanislavsky at the Moscow Arts Theater in 1909, are his most celebrated and characteristic. Like Benois, Doboujinsky was able to reconstruct an historical environment; like Benois, he tended to use decoration as decoration — that is, as a surface, static device. Doboujinsky's several versions of the sets for the Diaghilev production of *Les Papillons* in Paris in 1914 (with Bakst)[11] and the Metropolitan Opera company's production of *Un Ballo in Maschera* in 1940[12] are characteristic of this approach, repeating the measured symmetry and stylization germane to the World of Art masters. Even his work for the Metropolitan Opera Company and for the American Ballet in the 1940s, such as *Ballet Imperial* of 1941,[13] display the same common sense and precision.

Alexandre Golovine was a fellow member of the World of Art whose artistic psychology was closer to that of Bakst than to that of Benois and Doboujinsky. His magnificent set for Rubinstein's production of *Orphée* in 1926 is among the prized possessions of The Fine Arts Museums. Like Bakst, Golovine regarded the stage as a dynamic, variable medium, and his sets, dependent upon elements of Jugendstil and Art Nouveau, swirl and dance in mosaics of color and sinuous lines. Ultimately, his approach was ornamental, and therefore open to criticism. Benois, for example, after viewing several productions designed by Golovine, commented, "Combinations of original and beautiful coloring would appear on the stage, but these combinations expressed either nothing at all, or else something absolutely out of keeping with the problem. Golovine's methods were not essentially theatrical... the artist's scenic pictures were somehow inconsistent with the action."[14] The decor for *Orphée,* for instance, is distant from the historical and thematic aspects of the opera. As a piece of dynamic spectacle, however, it is magnificent. Perhaps for this reason the artist wrote, "I consider *Orphée* to be my most successful decor in opera, at least my favorite."[15]

A New Primitivism
In 1905 Stanislavsky founded his Theater Studio, an experimental workshop for the preparations of a new repertoire for the Moscow Arts Theater. With his assistant, Vsevolod Meierkhold, Stanislavsky concentrated on the Symbolist dramaturgy of Ibsen, Maeterlinck and others and invited a number of young painters to participate — painters who were outside the mainstream of the World of Art group. When, after only a few months, the Theater Studio closed and Meierkhold moved to Vera Komissarzhevskaia's theater in St. Petersburg, two important artists — Nikolai Sapunov and Sergei Soudeikine — followed, contributing to a number of novel productions there. Soudeikine, in particular, played an appreciable role in the development of modern Russian stage design, especially after 1910, the date of his decor and costumes for Meierkhold's production of the comedy *The Transformed Prince*.

A distinctive feature of Soudeikine's stage designs was intense stylization. While suitable to cabaret performances at Balieff's Chauve-Souris in Moscow, Berlin, Paris and New York, it did not always enhance ballets and operas. Soudeikine's costumes for *Petrouchka* (1925) and for *Le Rossignol* (1926), for example, might seem too static to function properly in such dynamic contexts. A primary source for his stylization was the Russian peasant toy as well as the *lubok* (a cheap, hand-colored broadside) and the icon. Soudeikine shared common ground with Gontcharova and Larionov, the leaders of the Neo-Primitivist movement, who also regarded such art forms — with their schematic animal and plant forms, their distorted perspective, their bright colors — as purer and more spontaneous than the methods peculiar to professional academic art.

Unlike Soudeikine, however, Gontcharova and Larionov were able to counter the stylization of primitive art with a remarkable gift for fantasy and playfulness. They, above all, were responsible for transforming the Russian stage into a buffoonery and for imbuing it with a new vitality and exuberance. Larionov, for example, returned the element of farce to the stage through the introduction of illogical, absurd and spontaneous elements. His designs for *Soleil du Nuit* (1915) and *Le Renard* (1922), or Gontcharova's for *Le Coq d'Or* (1914), *L'Oiseau de Feu* (1926) and *Chota Roustaveli* (1946), depend for their effect on a tension between narrative sequence and "displacement" (a favorite term of the Russian avant-garde poets and artists).[16] Larionov's many versions of the single set for *Le Renard*[17] express the very essence of this ingenuous burlesque about a cockerel, a fox, a cat and a ram who dance, sing and mime on an improvised platform outside a Russian hut in winter. The conception is simple, unadorned and functional, providing the bare necessities for the action and extending the mood of Stravinsky's candid, humorous music.

Perhaps Gontcharova remembered Larionov's *Le Renard* in her curtain, sets and costumes for *Chota Roustaveli*, a ballet choreographed by Serge Lifar and based on a fairy tale by the classical Georgian poet. Her designs, through their restraint and economy, convey the hieratic, pristine quality of the sparse Georgian landscape, just as Larionov's for *Le Renard* express the simplicity of the world of the Russian peasant. Gontcharova also joined forces with Stravinsky in her decor and costumes for the Diaghilev revival of *L'Oiseau de Feu* in 1926.[18] In the backdrop design she breaks the expected sequence of the churches by piling them one on top of the other, using them, therefore, not as the architectural description of a certain city but as a geometric pattern — a method that integrates with the staccato, angular composition of Stravinsky's music. Gontcharova's calculated, intellectual rendering of *L'Oiseau de Feu* was very different from the electrifying designs of Bakst and Golovine for the original production in 1910 and from her own Neo-Primitivist interpretation of *Le Coq d'Or* in 1914, surely her most theatrical and outrageous design. The Fine Arts Museums are fortunate to possess a project for a set from the first act of *Le Coq d'Or* (Cat. 62) which, like the variations in private and public collections,[19] demonstrates Gontcharova's debt to the *lubok*, the primitive painted tray, the signboard and the carved woodwork of the *izba*. Paris audiences, bewildered and stunned by the strident colors, applauded wildly when the curtain rose on *Le Coq d'Or* on May 21, 1914. The modest Benois was even rather insulted: "Least of all did I like the protrusion of her scenery which seemed even to impede the action."[20] No doubt Benois preferred the careful, illustrative designs that his World of Art colleague, Ivan Bilibin, did for Victor Zimin's Moscow production of *Le Coq d'Or* in 1909. Gontcharova had left Benois and Bilibin far behind.

Avant-Garde Trends
The productions of *La Légende de Joseph*, *Les Papillons* and *Le Coq d'Or*, all of 1914 and all presented by Diaghilev's Ballets Russes, testified to the energy and diversity of that enterprise. They also signified the end of the first and perhaps most memorable phase of the Ballets Russes. Thereafter, Diaghilev invited an increasing number of non-Russian artists to contribute to his ballets, including Pablo Picasso for *Parade* (1917), Laurencin for *Les Biches* (1924) and Pedro Pruna for *Les Matelots* (1925). Conversely, his original Russian artists began to work for other ballet companies. Diaghilev's monopoly of the Russian and European stage was brief and less exclusive than general opinion would have us believe. Exciting, innovative stage design was confined neither to the Diaghilev company nor to Paris.

Alexandra Exter, who never worked for Diaghilev, was a pioneer in experimental stage design. She was among the few members of the Russian avant-garde who succeeded in transcending the confines of the pictorial surface and in arranging forms in their interaction with space. This style was already evident, for example, in her first collaborations with Tairov on the productions of *Thamira Khytharedes* (1916) and *Salome* (1917) and then in her later undertakings such as *Romeo and Juliet* (1921). When the critic Yakov Tugendkhold wrote of *Thamira Khytharedes* that Tairov and Exter had endeavored to "make an organic connection between the moving actors and the objects at rest" and had resorted to the "dynamic use of immobile form,"[21] he was already anticipating the direction that Exter would follow. Exter's attention to the rhythmic organization of space forecasts her exuberant Constructivist designs of the 1920s for the stage, for the movie *Aelita* (1924), for textiles and for marionettes. Her set of hand-colored silkscreens, *Décors de Théâtre* of 1930 (Cat. 59), contains fifteen Constructivist maquettes, most of which remained as prototypes only, but all of which were in advance of their time. As the projects for *Othello* (1927) and *Revue Bateaux* (1930) indicate, Exter, along with Gontcharova and Nina Popova, was one of the few stage designers of the twentieth century able to think in terms of two and three dimensions. Exter passed on this plastic sense to some of her students, not least to Pavel Tchelitchew, represented in this collection by designs for Victor Zimin's productions in Istanbul in 1921 (Cats. 92, 93).

Diaghilev's Ballets Russes preceded the establishment of many private and public companies in later years, some of them ephemeral, others more enduring, and designers such as Bakst, Benois, Doboujinsky, Gontcharova and Soudeikine played formative roles in their development. Bakst and Golovine worked with Rubinstein; the Opéra Privé de Mme. Kousnetsov involved Bilibin, Alexis Korovine and others, and de Basil's Ballet Russe de Monte Carlo employed Benois, Gontcharova and others. Russian artists also contributed to the well-being of more illustrious institutions such as the Metropolitan Opera Company, New York, and the Teatro alla Scala, Milan. The Fine Arts Museums of San Francisco possess sets and costumes for several important productions relating to these theaters, for example, for *Le Rossignol* of 1926 by Soudeikine (Cats. 85–89) and *Un Ballo in Maschera* of 1940 by Doboujinsky (Cats. 55, 56), both at the Metropolitan, and for *Les Dryades* of 1953 by Bouchène at La Scala (Cats. 46–50).

Conclusion
One might argue that the companies and productions subsequent to the Ballets Russes never recaptured the true artistic synthesis that Diaghilev and his dancers and

designers managed to attain. On the other hand, these enterprises did enable a younger generation of Russians to maintain and expand the artistic contribution of their mentors to the international stage. Artists such as Berman, Bouchène, Alexandre Jacovleff and Simon Lissim developed the principles of Bakst and Benois, Exter and Gontcharova, upholding the primary traditions of the silver age of Russian culture. In collaboration with George Balanchine, Fokine, Boris Kochno, Lifar, Léonide Massine, such artists paid homage to their Russian heritage while communicating constantly with the representatives of many nations.

Few eyewitnesses of the Ballets Russes and the later companies survive. Suddenly that era has become historic, and the organic connection between these stage designs and their material environment has been obscured. We now tend to regard the sets and costumes of Bakst, Benois, Doboujinsky, Exter, Gontcharova, Lissim and their colleagues as pictures on the wall, as "works of art." They provide an intense visual delight independent of their original function — the clearest indication of their permanent artistic value.

John E. Bowlt
Director
The Institute of Modern Russian Culture
at Blue Lagoon, Texas

Notes

1. A list of exhibitions can be found in the Bibliography.

2. The Stravinsky-Diaghilev Foundation, New York, directed by Mrs. Parmenia Ekstrom, has not yet published a record of its holdings, although it has contributed frequently to exhibitions. The Wadsworth Atheneum collection of stage designs relies upon the Serge Lifar Collection (see *Lifar*, 1965, in Frequently Cited References). Mr. and Mrs. Nikita D. Lobanov have contributed works from their collections to many exhibitions and have organized five exhibitions drawing from their collections (see Bibliography and Frequently Cited References). Robert Tobin has also contributed to many exhibitions and organized his show *Explosion: Color: Paris 1909* in 1969. The Dance Collection of the New York Public Library has been cataloged and published. See *Dictionary Catalog of the Dance Collection* (Boston: Hall, 1974) in 10 volumes. Donald Oenslager published some of his holdings as *Stage Design* (New York: Viking, 1975).

3. Versions of Benois's backdrop for Armide's garden (Paris, 1909) are in the Wadsworth Atheneum and the Lobanov-Rostovsky Collection. Versions of the Ballerina (Paris, 1911) are in the Russian Museum, Leningrad, and the Wadsworth Atheneum.

4. A second version of the decor for *Hélène de Sparte* is in the Musée des Arts Décoratifs, Paris. The original maquette for the Doboujinsky set for *Les Papillons* (Paris, 1914) is in a private collection in Paris.

5. V. Kozlinsky and E. Freze, *Khudozhnik i teatr* (Moscow, 1975), p. 100.

6. A. Benois, *Memoirs* (London: Chatto and Windus, 1964), vol. 2, p. 235.

7. "Ida Rubinshtein o sebe," in *Solntse Rossii* (St. Petersburg, 1913), No. 25, p. 12.

8. L. Bakst, *Serov i ia v Gretsii* (Berlin: Slovo, 1923), p. 19.

9. Bakst expressed his views on *Hélène de Sparte* and his concept of Greece in an interview with Louis de Basilly, "A propos d'Hélène de Sparte" in *Siècle,* Paris, May 13, 1912. Quoted in I. Pruzhan, *Bakst* (Leningrad, 1975), p. 181.

10. Seven versions of Potiphar's Wife are in the collection of John Carr Doughty, Nottingham, England. Another version is in the Russian Museum, Leningrad.

11. Versions of the sets for the 1914 production are in the Wadsworth Atheneum, the Bakhrushin Museum, Moscow, and a private collection, Paris.

12. Designs for the 1940 production of *Un Ballo in Maschera* are in the collections of The New York Public Library and Vsevolod Doboujinsky, New York.

13. Designs for the 1941 production of *Ballet Imperial* are in the collections of the New York Public Library and The Museum of Modern Art, New York.

14. A. Benois, *Reminiscences of the Russian Ballet* (London: Putnam, 1941), p. 199.

15. A. Movshenson, ed., *Alexandr Yakovlevich Golovin. Vstrechi i vpechatleniia. Pisma. Vospominaniia o Golovine* (Leningrad–Moscow, 1960), p. 132.

16. The Futurist poet Alexei Kruchenykh wrote a book about the notion of "shift" or "displacement." See his *Sdvigologiia russkogo stikha* (Moscow, 1923).

17. Versions of the set for *Le Renard* (1922, 1929) are in collections of John Carr Doughty, Mme. A. Larionov, the Wadsworth Atheneum, Mr. and Mrs. Nikita D. Lobanov, and Boris Kochno.

18. Among the pieces connected with *L'Oiseau de Feu* in the Museums' collection is a costume for the First Prince (Cat. 64). The drawing would be associated with the First and Second Princes of *Le Coq d'Or* were it not for Gontcharova's inscription. Gontcharova herself may have confused the issue.

19. Versions of the set for the first act in *Le Coq d'Or* are in the collections of Evelyn Courand, Robert Tobin, the Bakhrushin Museum and others.

20. A. Benois, "Vospominaniia o balete,' in *Russkie zapiski* (Paris, 1939), No. 18, p. 101.

21. Ya. Tugendkhold, "Pismo iz Moskvy," in *Apollon* (Petrograd, 1917), No. 1, p. 72.

The Catalogue

Frequently Cited References

The American Federation of Arts, 1959–60

Fifty Years of Ballet Design, catalogue to an exhibition organized by the John Herron Art Museum, Indianapolis, Indiana (March 22 – April 19, 1959) in association with the Wadsworth Atheneum, Hartford, Connecticut (May 3 – May 22, 1959) and the California Palace of the Legion of Honor, San Francisco, California (July 11 – August 16, 1959). Circulated by The American Federation of Arts, New York, New York, September 1959 – September 1960.

Bulletin of the California Palace of the Legion of Honor, 1958

James I. Rambo, "A Gallery of the Dance. A Note on Recent Accessions," *Bulletin of the California Palace of the Legion of Honor,* July, 1958.

Bulletin of the California Palace of the Legion of Honor, 1959

James I. Rambo, "A Gallery of the Dance. A Note on Further Accessions," *Bulletin of the California Palace of the Legion of Honor,* September and October, 1959.

Dance Magazine, February, 1970

Olga Maynard, "Petrouchka, Diaghilev's 1911, Joffrey's 1970," *Dance Magazine,* February, 1970, pp. 47–61.

Diaghilev and Russian Stage Designers, 1972

Diaghilev and Russian Stage Designers, catalogue to an exhibition of stage and costume designs from the Lobanov-Rostovsky Collection. Circulated by the International Exhibitions Foundation, Washington, D.C., 1972–74.

Lifar, 1965

The Serge Lifar Collection of Ballet Set and Costume Designs, in the Wadsworth Atheneum, Hartford, Connecticut, published by the Wadsworth Atheneum on the occasion of the opening of Harkness House for Ballet Arts, New York, New York, November, 1965.

Russian Painters and the Stage, 1884–1965, 1977.

Russian Painters and the Stage, 1884–1965, catalogue to an exhibition of stage and costume designs from the Lobanov-Rostovsky Collection, held at the University Art Museum, The University of Texas at Austin, February 13 – March 13, 1977. Circulated by The University of Texas Art Museum, 1978–79.

Russian Stage and Costume Designs, 1967

Russian Stage and Costume Designs for the Ballet, Opera and Theatre, catalogue to an exhibition of stage and costume designs from the Lobanov-Rostovsky, Oenslager and Riabov Collections. Circulated by the International Exhibitions Foundation, 1967–69.

The Society of the Four Arts, 1976

The Golden Age of Ballet Design, catalogue to an exhibition held at The Society of Four Arts, Palm Beach, Florida, February 6 – March 7, 1976.

Notes to the Catalogue

The entries in this catalogue are arranged alphabetically by artist; designs by the same artist are chronologically ordered and grouped according to the productions for which they were made. When more than one production is listed for a ballet, opera or drama, the production that pertains to the designs in this collection is listed last.

A *project,* when it refers to a ballet, opera or drama, is a production that was never realized; when it refers to a decor or costume, it is a design that was executed for a particular production but never used.

Inscriptions, except those in Russian, have been transcribed without modification and appear in italics in the entries. Russian inscriptions have been translated into English and are not italicized.

Western spellings of artists' names agree with signatures and inscriptions found on works in this collection. Otherwise, when a traditional or personally favored form of spelling for a Russian name exists, this form has been used. Variant spellings are listed in the Bibliography.

Dimensions are given to the nearest sixteenth of an inch; height precedes width.

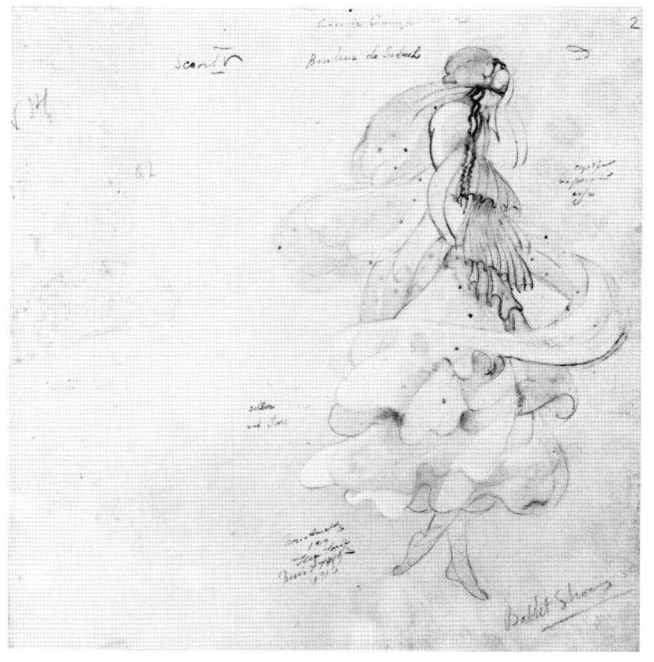

Boris Anisfeldt

Bieltsy, Bessarabia 1879–1973 New Canaan, Connecticut

The Bluebird

Opera in four acts

Libretto: Maurice Maeterlinck
Music: Albert Wolff

First produced by the Metropolitan Opera Company, New York, December 27, 1919

1 *Costume for a Dancing Girl, Bonheur du Soleil, Scene IV*

Pencil and watercolor on paper, 333 × 302 mm. (13⅛ × 11⅞ in.)
Signed, lower left, in red ink: *Boris Anisfeldt /1919 /*[illegible] *1919;* below this, in pencil: *Boris Anisfeldt /1919*
Inscribed, throughout, in pencil (in Russian): instructions to the dressmaker
Provenance: Sotheby's, London, December 15, 1969, lot 45; Sotheby's (Belgravia), London, November 17, 1971, lot 32

Gift of Mr. and Mrs. Nikita D. Lobanov, 1977.1TD

Léon Bakst

Grodno 1886–1924 Paris

Le Coeur de la Marquise

Pantomime

Music: E. Guirand
Choreography: Marius Petipa

First produced at the Hermitage Theater, St. Petersburg, February 22, 1902

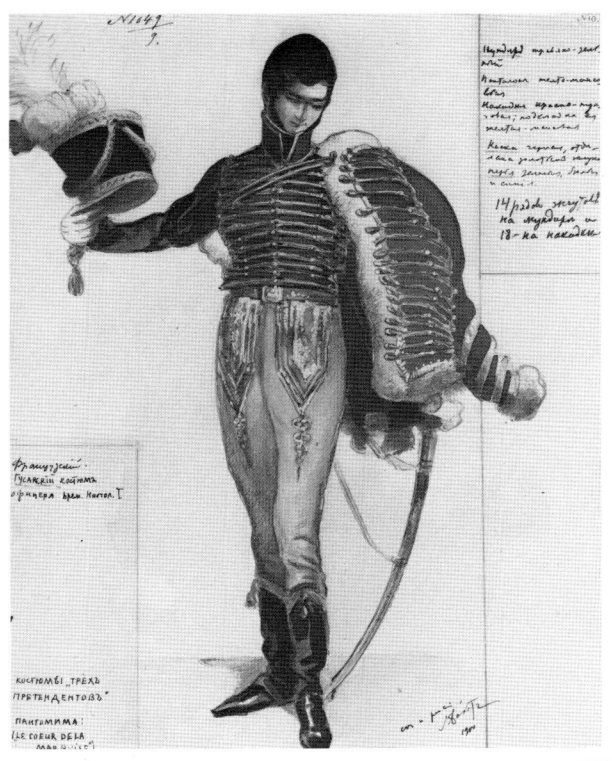

2 *Costume for the Three Pretenders*

Pencil and watercolor on paper, 295 × 225 mm. (11⅝ × 8⅞ in.)

Signed, lower right, in ink (in Russian): Composed and drawn by/L Bakst/*1900*

Inscribed, upper left, in ink: *N1049 / 9;* upper right, in ink (in Russian): instructions to the dressmaker; lower left, in ink (in Russian): French Hussar Uniform for an officer during the epoch of Napoleon I; below this, in ink (in Russian): Costumes for the Three Pretenders in the pantomime; below this, in ink: *("Le Coeur de la Marquise")*

Exhibitions: The Society of the Four Arts, 1976, No. 2

Bibliography: *Bulletin of the California Palace of the Legion of Honor,* 1958, repr.

Gift of Mrs. Adolph B. Spreckels, 1962.34TD

3 *Costume for the Woman Who Speaks the Prologue and the Epilogue*

Pencil and watercolor on paper, 295 × 229 mm. (11⅝ × 9 in.)

Signed, lower left, in ink: *Comp*[osé] *et dess*[iné]/*par L. Bakst*

Inscribed, upper left, in ink: *No. 1049 / 1;* upper right, in ink: *No. 1;* to the left of the figure, in ink: instructions to the dressmaker; across bottom, in ink: *LA JEUNE FILLE QUI DIT LE PROLOGUE ET L'EPILOGUE (MLLE. BALETTA)*

Exhibition: The Society of the Four Arts, 1976, No. 1

Gift of Mrs. Adolph B. Spreckels, 1962.35TD

4 *Costume for the Viscount Holding a Stick*

Pencil and watercolor on paper, 280 × 178 mm. (11 × 7 in.)

Signed, lower right, in ink (in Russian): Composed and drawn/by L Bakst/*1900*

Inscribed, lower left, in ink (in Russian): Costume for the Viscount/ Pantomime *"Le Coeur de la Marquise";* to the right of the figure, in ink (in Russian): instructions to the dressmaker

Exhibition: The Society of the Four Arts, 1976, No. 3

Gift of Mrs. Adolph B. Spreckels, 1962.39TD

Schéhérazade

Choreographic drama in one act

Scenario: Alexandre Benois
Music: Nicholas Rimsky-Korsakov
Choreography: Michel Fokine

First produced by Sergei Diaghilev[1] at the Théâtre National de l'Opéra, Paris, June 4, 1910

[1]. Productions produced by Diaghilev were performed by the Ballets Russes, the company he founded in 1909 and directed until his death in 1929.

5 *Costume for the Sultan Zeman* (with design for one slipper)

Pencil, watercolor and gold paint on paper, 305 × 235 mm. (12 × 9¼ in.)
Signed, lower right, in pencil: *Bakst*
Exhibition: The Society of the Four Arts, 1976, No. 13

Gift of Mrs. Adolph B. Spreckels, 1962.45TD

Hélène de Sparte

Tragedy in four acts

Author: Émile Verhaeren
Music: Déodat de Séverac

First produced by Ida Rubinstein in association with the Société Musicale de Gavriel Astruc at the Théâtre du Châtelet, Paris, May 4, 1912

6 *Decor, Acts I and III*

Watercolor on paper, 810 × 1,165 mm. (31¾ × 45¾ in.)
Signed, lower right, in pencil: *Bakst*

Gift of Mrs. Adolph B. Spreckels, 1962.37TD

Another version of this decor is in the collection of the Musée des Arts Décoratifs, Paris (*Diaghilev et Les Ballets Russes,* catalogue to an exhibition held at the Bibliothèque Nationale, Paris, 1979, No. 136).

 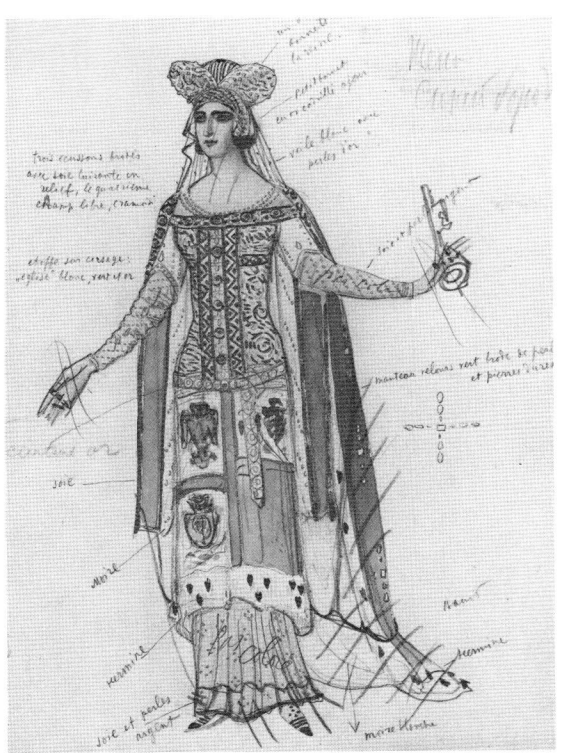 

Daphnis et Chloë

Ballet in one act, three scenes

Scenario: Michel Fokine
Music: Maurice Ravel
Choreography: Michel Fokine

First produced by Sergei Diaghilev at the Théâtre du Châtelet, Paris, June 8, 1912

7 *Costume for a Warrior*

Pencil, watercolor and silver paint on paper, 270×162 mm. (10⅝×6⅜ in.)
Signed, lower right, in pencil: *Bakst*
Inscribed, upper right, in pencil: *"Daphnis et Chloë" /6 guerriers*
Exhibitions: The Society of the Four Arts, 1976, No. 12
Bibliography: *Bulletin of the California Palace of the Legion of Honor,* 1959, repr.

Gift of Mrs. Adolph B. Spreckels, 1962.47TD

La Pisanella ou la Morte Parfumée

Drama

Author: Gabriele d'Annunzio
Music: Ildebrando Pizzetti
Choreography: Michel Fokine

First produced by Vsevolod Meierkhold for Ida Rubinstein at the Théâtre du Châtelet, Paris, June 11, 1913

8 *Costume for the Wife of the Blue Bird*

Pencil, watercolor, and silver and gold paint on paper, 352×251 mm. (13⅞×9⅞ in.)
Signed, lower right, in pencil: *Bakst*
Inscribed, throughout, in pencil: instructions to the dressmaker

Gift of Mrs. Adolph B. Spreckels, 1962.42TD

9 *Costume for the Queen, Prologue*

Pencil, watercolor and gold paint on paper, 349×241 mm. (13¾×9½ in.)
Signed, lower right, in pencil: *Bakst*
Inscribed, upper right, in pencil: *Pisanella Prologue / La Reine (Mme Suzanne Munte) / 1 costume riche;* to the right of the figure, in pencil: instructions to the dressmaker
Exhibition: The Society of the Four Arts, 1976, No. 4
Bibliography: *Bulletin of the California Palace of the Legion of Honor,* 1959, repr.

Gift of Mrs. Adolph B. Spreckels, 1962.41TD

10 *Costume for a Nestor*

Pencil, watercolor and gold paint on paper, 298×210 mm. (11¾×8¼ in.)
Signed, lower right, in pencil: *Bakst*
Inscribed, upper right, in pencil: *Pisanella / I acte / Nestoriens / 4 costumes*
Exhibition: The Society of the Four Arts, 1976, No. 6

Gift of Mrs. Adolph B. Spreckels, 1962.44TD

La Légende de Joseph

Ballet in one act

Scenario: Harry von Kessler and Hugo von Hofmannsthal
Music: Richard Strauss
Decor: José-Maria Sert
Choreography: Michel Fokine

First produced by Sergei Diaghilev at the Théâtre National de l'Opéra, Paris, May 17, 1914

11 *Costume for Potiphar's Wife* (danced by Maria Kousnetsov)

Pencil, watercolor and gold paint on paper, 483×330 mm. (19×13 in.)
Signed, lower right, in pencil: *Bakst*
Exhibitions: The American Federation of Arts, 1959–60, No. 19; The Society of the Four Arts, 1976, No. 11

Gift of Mrs. Adolph B. Spreckels, 1959.38TD

Seven versions of this costume are in the collection of John Carr Doughty, Nottingham, England. Another version is in the Russian Museum, Leningrad.

The Sleeping Princess (La Belle au Bois Dormant)

Ballet in a prologue and three acts
Scenario: Marius Petipa and Ivan Vsevolojsky, after the story by Charles Perrault
Music: Peter Tchaikovsky
Choreography: Marius Petipa
First produced at the Mariinsky Theater, St. Petersburg, January 3, 1890
Produced by Sergei Diaghilev at the Alhambra Theater, London, November 2, 1921

12 *Costume for a Minister of State, Scene I*

Pencil, gouache and gold paint on paper, 302 × 292 mm. (11⅞ × 9 in.)
Signed, lower right, in pencil: *Bakst*
Inscribed, upper right, in pencil: *Reception au / Jardin du Sultan / Un Ministre*
Exhibition: The Society of the Four Arts, 1976, No. 7

Gift of Mrs. Adolph B. Spreckels, 1962.43TD

13 *Costume for a Jewish Dancer and a Black Slave*

Pencil, crayon and watercolor on paper, 622 × 470 mm. (24⅝ × 18½ in.)
Signed, lower right, in ink: *Bakst / 1921*
Exhibition: The Society of the Four Arts, 1976, No. 10 (as *Design for Unidentified Production, Figure sketch: woman with veils*)

Gift of Mrs. Adolph B. Spreckels, 1962.40TD

Bakst based this drawing on one of his original designs for the ballet *Cléopâtre,* produced by Sergei Diaghilev at the Théâtre du Châtelet, Paris, in 1909.

Judith

Opera

Libretto: Alexandre Serov and Apollon Maikov
Music: Alexandre Serov
Decors: Valentin Serov

First produced in St. Petersburg, May 28, 1863
Produced by Ida Rubinstein, Paris, 1922

Judith

Drama in three acts, seven scenes

Author: Henri Bernstein
Decors: Sergei Soudeikine

First produced by Alexandre Antoine at the Théâtre du Gymnase, Paris, October, 1922

Bakst's first costumes for *Judith* were executed in 1909 for Diaghilev's production of the opera by Serov. In 1922

Bakst designed costumes for another production of the opera as well as for a play of the same title by Bernstein. Without accurate production data it is not possible to distinguish designs for the opera of 1922 from those of the play.

14 *Costume for an Old Jew Holding the Head of Holofernes*

Pencil, watercolor and silver paint on paper, 445×273 mm. (17⅜×10¾ in.)
Signed, lower left, in watercolor: *Bakst /22*

Gift of Mrs. Adolph B. Spreckels, 1962.36TD

15 *Costume for Judith*

Pencil, watercolor and silver paint on paper, 479×302 mm. (18⅞×11⅞ in.)
Signed, lower right, in watercolor: *Bakst /1922*
Exhibition: The Society of the Four Arts, No. 9

Gift of Mrs. Adolph B. Spreckels, 1962.38TD

Alexandre Benois

St. Petersburg 1870– 1960 Paris

Le Pavillon d'Armide

Ballet-pantomime in one act, three scenes
Scenario: Alexandre Benois, from Théophile Gautier's story *Omphale*
Music: Nicholas Tchérépnine
Choreography: Michel Fokine

First produced at the Mariinsky Theater, St. Petersburg, November 25, 1907
Produced by Sergei Diaghilev at the Théâtre du Châtelet, Paris, 1909

16 *Backdrop for Armide's Garden (Dream Scene), Scene II*

Pencil, pen and ink, and watercolor on paper, 219 × 281 mm. (8⅝ × 11¼ in.)

Signed, lower left, in ink: *Alexandre Benois*
Inscribed, lower right, in pencil: *Le Pavillon d'Armide II*
Exhibition: The Society of the Four Arts, 1976, No. 15

Gift of Mrs. Adolph B. Spreckels, 1962.83TD

Other versions of this backdrop are in the Lifar Collection, Wadsworth Atheneum (*Lifar,* 1965, No. 17, repr.), and the Lobanov-Rostovsky Collection (*Diaghilev and Russian Stage Designers,* 1972, No. 12, repr.).

17 *Costume for the Old Marquis, Scene III*

Pencil, pen and ink, and watercolor on paper, 311 × 235 mm. (12¼ × 9¼ in.)
Signed, lower right, in pencil: *Alexandre/ Benois/1909*
Inscribed, upper left, in pencil: *Le Pavillon / d'Armide /1909;* upper right, in pencil: *Le Marquis /IIIème tableau*
Exhibitions: The American Federation of Arts, 1959– 60, No. 73; The Society of the Four Arts, 1976, No. 16

Gift of Mrs. Adolph B. Spreckels, 1962.32TD

Another version of this costume is in the Lifar Collection, Wadsworth Atheneum (*Lifar,* 1965, No. 18, repr.).

Petrouchka

Burlesque ballet in one act, four scenes

Scenario: Igor Stravinsky and Alexandre Benois
Music: Igor Stravinsky
Choreography: Michel Fokine

First produced by Sergei Diaghilev at the Théâtre du Châtelet, Paris, June 13, 1911
Produced by the Opera House, Vienna, 1956

18 *Program Cover with Decor for Act I, Scenes I and IV*

Pencil and watercolor on paper, 317 × 241 mm. (12½ × 9½ in.)
Signed, lower right, in ink: *Alexandre Benois 1955*
Provenance: Boris Kochno
Exhibition: The Society of the Four Arts, 1976, No. 29

Gift of Mrs. Adolph B. Spreckels, 1959.42TD

Benois based this program cover of 1956 on the one he designed for the original production of 1911. The translation of the Russian is as follows: Petrouchka / Burlesque activities in four parts / Composed by Igor Stravinsky and Alexandre Benois / Music by Igor Stravinsky / Paris / 1911.

19 *Costume for the Ballerina* (danced by Tamara Karsavina)

Pencil, pen and ink, watercolor and gold paint on paper, 305 × 225 mm. (12 × 8⅞ in.)
Signed, lower right, in pencil: *Alexandre / Benois*
Inscribed, upper left, in pencil: *La Ballerine / pour / Mme. Karsavina*
Exhibitions: The American Federation of Arts, 1959–60, No. 92; The Society of the Four Arts, 1976, No. 31

Gift of Mrs. Adolph B. Spreckels, 1959.46TD

Other versions of this costume are in the Lobanov-Rostovsky Collection (*Dance Magazine*, February, 1970, repr. pp. 54–55), the Lifar Collection, Wadsworth-Atheneum (*Lifar*, 1965, No. 32, repr.), and the Russian Museum, Leningrad.

20 *Costume for Petrouchka* (danced by Vaslav Nijinsky)

Pencil, pen and ink, and watercolor on paper, 305×225 mm. (12×8⅞ in.)
Signed, lower left, in pencil: *Alexandre / Benois*
Inscribed, upper left, in pencil: *Petrouchka / création / en 1911;* upper right, in pencil: *Petrouchka / M. W. Nijinsky*
Exhibitions: The American Federation of Arts, 1959–60, No. 92; The Society of the Four Arts, 1976, No. 30

Gift of Mrs. Adolph B. Spreckels, 1959.48TD

Other versions of this costume are in the Lifar Collection, Wadsworth Atheneum (*Lifar,* 1965, No. 31, repr.), and the Lobanov-Rostovsky Collection (*Dance Magazine,* February, 1970, repr. p. 55).

21 *Costume for the Man with the Peep Show*

Pencil, pen and ink and watercolor on paper, 302×238 mm. (11¾×9⅜ in.)
Signed, lower left, in pencil: *Alexandre / Benois*
Inscribed, upper left, in pencil: *Petrouchka / 1911;* upper right, in pencil: *Le Montreur / d'"Optiques" / et des / Enfants au / peuple*
Provenance: Boris Kochno
Exhibitions: The American Federation of Arts, 1959–60, No. 92; The Society of the Four Arts, 1976, No. 35

Gift of Mrs. Adolph B. Spreckels, 1959.45TD

Another version of this costume is in the Lobanov-Rostovsky Collection (*Dance Magazine,* February, 1970, repr. p. 51).

22 *Costume for the Moor* (danced by Alexander Orloff)

Pencil, pen and ink, and watercolor on paper, 305×241 mm. (12×19½ in.)
Signed, lower left, in pencil: *Alexandre / Benois*
Inscribed, upper left, in pencil: *"Petrouchka / 1911";* upper right, in pencil: *Le Nègre / M. Orloff*
Provenance: Boris Kochno
Exhibitions: The American Federation of Arts, 1959–60, No. 92; The Society of the Four Arts, 1976, No. 32

Gift of Mrs. Adolph B. Spreckels, 1959.43TD

Other versions of this costume are in the collection of the Arts Council of Great Britain, London (The American Federation of Arts, 1959–60, No. 86, repr.), and the Lobanov-Rostovsky Collection (*Dance Magazine,* February, 1970, repr. p. 54).

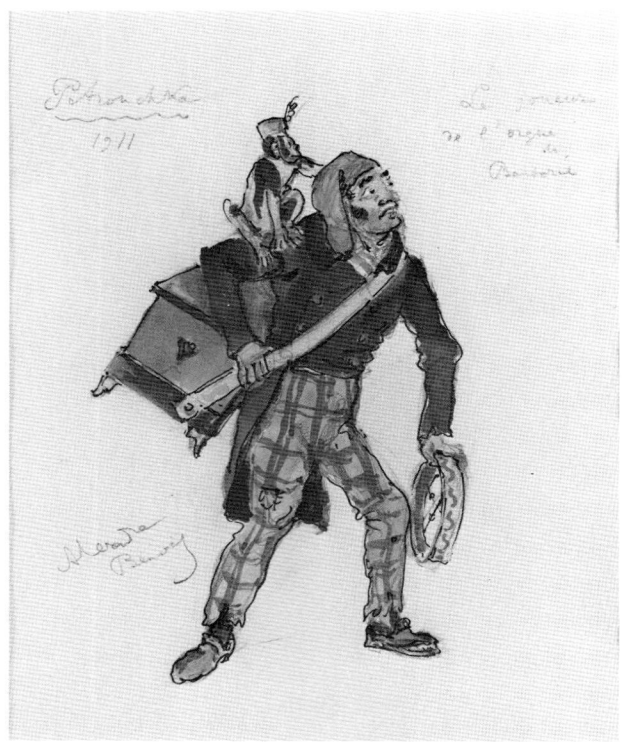  

23 *Costume for the Organ Grinder and Monkey*

Pencil, pen and ink, and watercolor on paper, 305 × 238 mm. (12 × 9⅜ in.)
Signed, lower left, in pencil: *Alexandre / Benois*
Inscribed, upper left, in pencil: *Petrouchka / 1911*; upper right, in pencil: *Le joueur / de l'orgue / et / Barbarie*
Provenance: Boris Kochno
Exhibition: The American Federation of Arts, 1959–60, No. 92

Gift of Mrs. Adolph B. Spreckels, 1959.49TD

24 *Costume for the Magician*

Pencil, pen and ink, and watercolor on paper, 305 × 238 mm. (12 × 9⅜ in.)
Signed, lower right, in pencil: *Alexandre / Benois*
Inscribed, upper right, in pencil: *Petrouchka / 1911*; upper left, in pencil: *Le Magicien / (Le Prestidigitateur) / the Conjuror*
Provenance: Boris Kochno, 1958
Exhibitions: The American Federation of Arts, 1959–60, No. 92; The Society of the Four Arts, 1976, No. 33

Gift of Mrs. Adolph B. Spreckels, 1959.47TD

Another version of this costume is in the Lobanov-Rostovsky Collection (*Dance Magazine,* February, 1970, repr. p. 50).

25 *Costume for the Drum Major and Four Children*

Pencil, pen and ink, and watercolor on paper, 305 × 228 mm. (12 × 9 in.)
Signed, lower right, in pencil: *Alexandre / Benois*
Inscribed, upper left, in pencil: *Petrouchka / Création 1911*; upper right, in pencil: *Le tambour major / du Régiment / Pavlovski / et des / enfants pauvres*
Provenance: Boris Kochno
Exhibitions: The American Federation of Arts, 1959–60, No. 92; The Society of the Four Arts, 1976, No. 34

Gift of Mrs. Adolph B. Spreckels, 1959.44TD

Giselle

Ballet-pantomime in two acts

Scenario: Vernoy de Saint-Georges, Théophile Gautier and Jean Coralli
Music: Adolph Adam
Choreography: Jean Coralli and Jules Perrot

First produced at the Théâtre de l'Académie Royale de Musique, Paris, June 28, 1841
Produced by Sergei Diaghilev at the Théâtre National de l'Opéra, Paris, June 18, 1910; revived by the Théâtre National de l'Opéra, Paris, 1924 and 1948

26 *Backdrop, Act I, with Giselle and Albrecht on stage*

Pen and ink, watercolor and gouache on paper, 479 × 613 mm. (18⅞ × 24⅛ in.)
Signed, lower left, in ink: *Alexandre Benois 1924*
Inscribed, lower left, in ink: *Giselle, Act I*; lower right, in ink: [illegible]
Exhibition: The Society of the Four Arts, 1976, No. 17

Gift of Mrs. Adolph B. Spreckels, 1962.103TD

Another version of this backdrop is in the Lifar Collection, Wadsworth Atheneum (*Lifar*, 1965, No. 33, repr.).

27 *Costume for Giselle* (danced by Tamara Karsavina)

Pencil, pen and ink, and watercolor on paper, 302 × 235 mm. (11⅞ × 9¼ in.)
Signed, lower left, in ink: *Alexandre / Benois*
Inscribed, upper left, in pencil: *Giselle / 1910*; upper right, in pencil: *Giselle / pour / Mme. Karsavina*; lower left, in ink: *pour / l'Opéra de Paris*
Exhibition: The Society of the Four Arts, 1976, No. 20

Gift of Mrs. Adolph B. Spreckels, 1962.84TD

Another version of this costume is in the Lifar Collection, Wadsworth Atheneum (*Lifar*, 1965, No. 37, repr.).

28 *Costume for Albrecht, Act I*

Pencil and watercolor on paper, 238×159 mm. (9⅜×6¼ in.)

Signed, lower right, in green pencil: *Alexandre / Benois*

Inscribed, upper left, in green pencil: *Giselle à l'Opéra*; lower left, in pencil: *V. 1948*; lower right, in pencil: *N 1.*

Exhibition: The Society of the Four Arts, 1976, No. 21

Gift of Mrs. Adolph B. Spreckels, 1962.87TD

29 *Backdrop for the Cemetery of the Wilis, Act II, with Albrecht standing in front of Giselle's grave*

Watercolor and gouache on paper, 346×572 mm. (13⅝×22½ in.)

Signed, lower left, in red chalk: *Alexandre / Benois / XII 1948*

Exhibition: The Society of the Four Arts, 1976, No. 18

Gift of Mrs. Adolph B. Spreckels, 1962.33TD

Another version of this backdrop (without the figure of Albrecht) is in the Lifar Collection, Wadsworth Atheneum (*Lifar,* 1965, No. 34, repr.)

30 *Costume for Albrecht in Mourning, Act II* (danced by Vaslav Nijinsky)

Pencil, pen and ink, and watercolor on paper, 251 × 200 mm. (9⅞ × 7⅞ in.)

Signed, lower left, in pencil: *Alexandre / Benois*

Inscribed, upper left, in pencil: *Giselle*; upper right, in pencil: *Le Prince / en / deuil / (IIème acte) / pour / M. Nijinksy*

Exhibition: The Society of the Four Arts, 1976, No. 22

Gift of Mrs. Adolph B. Spreckels, 1962.70TD

31 *Backdrop for the Cemetery of the Wilis, Act II, with Albrecht standing in front of Giselle's grave*

Pen and ink, watercolor and gouache on paper, 499 × 649 mm. (19⅞ × 25¾ in.)

Signed, lower right, in red chalk: *Alexandre / Benois / XI 1948*

Exhibition: The Society of the Four Arts, 1976, No. 19 (incorrectly described as unsigned)

Gift of Mrs. Adolph B. Spreckels, 1962.102TD

32 *Costume for a Nobleman at the Hunt*

Pencil, pen and ink, and watercolor on paper, 232 × 178 mm. (9¼ × 7 in.)
Inscribed, in pencil, upper left: *Giselle / 1949 / pour Paris*; upper right, in pencil: *Seigneur à la chasse*; lower right, in pencil: *N 5*.

Gift of Mrs. Adolph B. Spreckels, 1962.72TD

33 *Costume for a Young Man*

Pencil and watercolor on paper, 241 × 159 mm. (9½ × 6¼ in.)
Signed, lower left, in pencil: *Alexandre / Benois*
Inscribed, upper left, in pencil: *Giselle 1949 / pour Paris*; upper right, in pencil: *Les / Amis de / Giselle*; lower left, in pencil: *V. 1948*; lower right, in pencil: *N 7*
Exhibition: The Society of the Four Arts, 1976, No. 28

Gift of Mrs. Adolph B. Spreckels, 1962.73TD

34 *Costume for Wilfrid, Act I*

Pencil, pen and ink, and watercolor on paper, 241 × 159 mm. (9½ × 6¼ in.)
Signed, lower right, in pencil: *Alexandre / Benois*
Inscribed, upper left, in pencil: *Giselle / 1949* (partially erased) */pour Milan*; upper right, in pencil: *Wilfrid / I*; lower left, in pencil: *V. 1948 / pour Milan*; lower right, in pencil: *N 6*
Exhibition: The Society of the Four Arts, 1976, No. 26

Gift of Mrs. Adolph B. Spreckels, 1962.89TD

35 *Costume for Hilarion*

Pencil, pen and ink, and watercolor, 235×172 mm. (9¼×6¾ in.)
Signed, lower left, in pencil: *Alexandre / Benois*
Inscribed, upper left, in pencil: *Giselle / 1949*; upper right, in pencil: *Hilarion / Costume / analogue / envoyé à / Milan / en 1950*; lower left: *V. 1948 / pour Paris*; lower right: *Giselle / N 3*
Exhibition: The Society of the Four Arts, 1976, No. 23

Gift of Mrs. Adolph B. Spreckels, 1962.85TD

36 *Costume for a Female Grape Picker*

Pencil, pen and ink, and watercolor on paper, 245×159 mm. (9⅝×6¼ in.)
Signed, lower right, in ink (over pencil): *Alexandre / Benois / 1949*
Inscribed, upper left, in pencil: *Giselle / 1949*; upper right, in pencil: *Les Vendangeuses / raisins*
Exhibition: The Society of the Four Arts, 1976, No. 24

Gift of Mrs. Adolph B. Spreckels, 1962.88TD

37 *Costume for a Court Attendant with Falcon*

Pencil and watercolor on paper, 241×159 mm. (9½×6¼ in.)
Signed, lower right, in pencil: *Alexandre Benois*
Inscribed, upper left, in pencil: *Giselle / 1949*; lower left, in pencil: *pour Paris / V. 1948*; lower right, in pencil: *N 8*
Exhibition: The Society of the Four Arts, 1976, No. 27

Gift of Mrs. Adolph B. Spreckels, 1962.86TD

38 *Costume for a Nobleman at the Hunt*

Pencil, pen and ink, and watercolor on paper, 232×178 mm. (9¼×7 in.)
Signed, lower right, in pencil: *Alexandre Benois*
Inscribed, upper left, in pencil: *Giselle/1949* (partially erased); upper right, in pencil: *Seigneur à la/chasse/Giselle/1949*; lower left, in pencil: *V./1948/pour Milan*; lower right, in pencil: *N 11.*
Exhibition: The Society of the Four Arts, 1976, No. 25

Gift of Mrs. Adolph B. Spreckels, 1962.90TD

Raymonda

Ballet in three acts, four scenes

Scenario: Lydia Pashkova and Marius Petipa
Music: Alexander Glazunov
Choreography: Marius Petipa

First produced at the Mariinsky Theater, St. Petersburg, January 7–19, 1898
Produced by the Ballet Russe de Monte Carlo[1] at the City Center Theater, New York, March 12, 1946

[1]. René Blum founded the Ballets Russes de Monte Carlo in 1931 and later directed it in partnership with Colonel Wassily de Basil. When Blum resigned in 1936, the company came under the sole directorship of de Basil. After its second season in 1933, it changed its name to the singular and became known as the Ballet Russe de Monte Carlo.

39 *Decor for the Duel Scene between the Knight and Jean de Brieune, Act II*

Pencil, pen and ink, and watercolor on paper, 305×470 mm. (12×18½ in.)
Signed, lower left, in ink: *Alexandre Benois*
Inscribed, lower right, in ink: *Ire esquisse de la Ire version du II acte de Raymonde/1945*
Exhibitions: The Society of the Four Arts, 1976, No. 37
Bibliography: *Bulletin of the California Palace of the Legion of Honor,* 1958, repr.

Gift of Mrs. Adolph B. Spreckels, 1962.31TD

Eugène Berman

St. Petersburg, 1899–1972 Rome

Icare

Neoclassic ballet in one act, two scenes

Scenario: Serge Lifar
Music (percussion arrangement): J. E. Szyfer
Choreography: Serge Lifar

First produced at the Théâtre National de l'Opéra, Paris, July 9, 1935
Produced by the Ballet Russe de Monte Carlo at the Metropolitan Opera House, New York, October 21, 1958

40 *Costume for Dedalus*

Pen and ink and watercolor on paper, 27×19 mm. (10½×7½ in.)
Inscribed, upper right, in ink: *Dedale*; lower right, in pencil: *Facecloth*; upper left, in pencil (in Russian): 4 yards/1 and 50 blue
Provenance: Ballet Russe de Monte Carlo

Gift of Mr. and Mrs. Nikita D. Lobanov, 1977.3TD

Le Bourgeois Gentilhomme

Ballet in two scenes

Scenario: George Balanchine
Music: Richard Strauss
Choreography: George Balanchine

First produced by the Ballet Russe de Monte Carlo at the City Center of Music and Drama, New York, 1944

41 *Costume for a Young Girl*

Pen and ink, watercolor and gouache on paper, 315×235 mm. (12½×9¼ in.)
Inscribed, across top, in ink: *Le Bourgeois Gentilhomme*; across bottom, in ink: *La Comédie Italienne*

Gift of Mr. and Mrs. Nikita D. Lobanov, 1977.4TD

Boris Bilinsky

near Odessa 1910– 1948 Catania, Sicily

L'Oiseau de Feu

Ballet in one act, two scenes

Scenario: Michel Fokine
Music: Igor Stravinsky
Choreography: Michel Fokine

First produced by Sergei Diaghilev at the Théâtre National de l'Opéra, Paris, June 25, 1910
Project, Paris, 1925

42 *Project for Decor*

Gouache and gold paint on paper, 335×490 mm. (12¾×19½ in.)
Signed, lower right, in gouache, with the artist's monogram and *25*
Gift of Mr. and Mrs. Nikita D. Lobanov, 1977.6TD

L'Amour Sorcier

Ballet in one act with voices

Music: Manuel de Falla
Choreography: Boris Romanov

Produced by the Ballets Russes de Monte Carlo, Paris, 1931

43 *Costume for the Chinaman*

Pen and ink, watercolor and gold paint on paper, 487×315 mm. (19¼×12¼ in.)
Signed, lower right, in pencil, with the artist's monogram
Provenance: Mrs. Boris Bilinsky

Gift of Mr. and Mrs. Nikita D. Lobanov, 1977.8TD

Prince Igor

Opera in a prologue and four acts

Libretto: Alexander Borodin and Vladimir Stasov
Music: Alexander Borodin

First produced at the Imperial Opera House, St. Petersburg, October 23, 1890
Project, Opéra Russe de Paris, 1932

44 *Costume for a Polovtsian Warrior*

Watercolor, gouache and gold paint on paper, 528×344 mm. (20¾×13½ in.)

Gift of Mr. and Mrs. Nikita D. Lobanov, 1977.7TD

La Princesse Cygne

Ballet

Music: Nicholas Rimsky-Korsakov
Choreography: Bronislava Nijinska

Produced by Bronislava Nijinka's Théâtre de Dance at the Théâtre National de l'Opéra Comique, Paris, 1932

45 *Costume for a Russian Peasant Woman*

Pencil and watercolor on paper, 500×325 mm. (19¾×12¾ in.)

Inscribed, lower left, in pencil (in Russian): Bread and Salt/No. 2; lower right, in pencil: *Le Pain et le Sel*

Provenance: Mrs. Boris Bilinsky

Gift of Mr. and Mrs. Nikita D. Lobanov, 1977.9TD

Another version of this costume is in the Lobanov-Rostovsky Collection (*Russian Painters and the Stage 1884–1965,* 1977, No. 28, repr.).

Dmitri Bouchène

St. Tropez 1898 – living in Paris

Les Dryades

Ballet

Music: Frédéric Chopin
Choreography: Léonide Massine

First produced at the Teatro dell'Opera, Rome, January 12, 1954

46 *Decor*

Gouache on paper, 241×312 mm. (9½×12⅜ in.)
Signed, lower right, in pencil: *Bouchène*
Inscribed, lower left, in pencil: *"Les Dryades" / Ballet*; lower right, in pencil: *Rome 1953*
Provenance: Acquired by Mrs. Adolph B. Spreckels from the artist, 1958
Exhibition: The Society of the Four Arts, 1976, No. 43

Gift of Mrs. Adolph B. Spreckels, 1962.4TD

47 *Costume for a Female Dancer*

Pencil and watercolor on paper, 316×242 mm. (12½×9⅜ in.)
Signed, lower left, in pencil: *Bouchène*
Inscribed, upper right, in pencil: *"Les Dryades" / Ballet*; lower right, in pencil: *Rome / 1953*
Provenance: Acquired by Mrs. Adolph B. Spreckels from the artist, 1958
Exhibition: The Society of the Four Arts, 1976, No. 46

Gift of Mrs. Adolph B. Spreckels, 1962.8TD

48 *Costume for a Male Figure as a Tree*

    Pencil and gouache on paper, 318 × 242 mm. (12⅜ × 9½ in.)
    Signed, lower right, in pencil: *Bouchène*
    Inscribed, lower left, in pencil: *"Les Dryades" / Ballet Rome / 1953*
    Provenance: Acquired by Mrs. Adolph B. Spreckels from the artist, 1958
    Exhibition: The Society of the Four Arts, 1976, No. 45

    Gift of Mrs. Adolph B. Spreckels, 1962.6TD

49 *Decor*

    Gouache on paper, 375 × 590 mm. (14¾ × 23¼ in.)
    Signed, lower right, in gouache: *Bouchène*
    Provenance: Acquired by Mrs. Adolph B. Spreckels from the artist, 1958
    Exhibition: The Society of the Four Arts, 1976, No. 42

    Gift of Mrs. Adolph B. Spreckels, 1962.5TD

50 *Costume for a Male Figure*

Pencil and gouache on paper, 314 × 242 mm. (12⅜ × 9½ in.)
Signed, lower right, in pencil: *Bouchène*
Inscribed, upper right, in pencil: *"Les Dryades" / Ballet / Rome 1953*
Provenance: Acquired by Mrs. Adolph B. Spreckels from the artist, 1958
Exhibition: The Society of the Four Arts, 1976, No. 44

Gift of Mrs. Adolph B. Spreckels, 1962.7TD

Aurora's Wedding

Ballet in one act (shortened version of *The Sleeping Princess*)

Music: Peter Tchaikovsky

Choreography: Serge Grigoriev (reconstruction after the original Sergei Diaghilev production, choreographed by Marius Petipa and Bronislava Nijinska)

First produced by Sergei Diaghilev at the Théâtre National de l'Opéra, Paris, May 18, 1922 (with decors by Léon Bakst and costumes by Alexandre Benois)

Produced at the Teatro alla Scala, Milan, 1956

51 *Costume for the Blue Bird*

Pencil and gouache on paper, 318 × 242 mm. (12⅜ × 9½ in.)
Signed, lower left, in pencil: *Bouchène*
Inscribed, upper left, in pencil: *"Le Nozze / di Aurora"*; upper right, in pencil: *Milano 1956 / Teatro alla Scala*; lower left, in pencil: *L'Oiseau / Bleu*
Provenance: Acquired by Mrs. Adolph B. Spreckels from the artist, 1958
Exhibition: The Society of the Four Arts, 1976, No. 41

Gift of Mrs. Adolph B. Spreckels, 1962.27TD

52 *Costume for a Dancer in "La Valse"*

Pencil and gouache on paper, 318 × 242 mm. (12½ × 9¼ in.)
Signed, lower right, in pencil: *Bouchène*
Inscribed, upper right, in pencil: *"Le Nozze / di Aurora" / La Valse*; lower left, in pencil: *Milano 1956 / Teatro alla Scala*
Provenance: Acquired by Mrs. Adolph B. Spreckels from the artist, 1958
Exhibition: The Society of the Four Arts, 1976, No. 40

Gift of Mrs. Adolph B. Spreckels, 1962.28TD

53 *Decor*

Gouache on paper, 327 × 584 mm. (12⅞ × 23 in.)
Signed, lower right, in gouache: *Bouchène*
Provenance: Acquired by Mrs. Adolph B. Spreckels from the artist, 1958

Gift of Mrs. Adolph B. Spreckels, 1962.26TD

Mstislav Doboujinsky

Nizhny-Novgorod 1875– 1957 New York

Les Papillons

Ballet in one act

Scenario: Michel Fokine
Music: Robert Schumann, orchestrated by Nicholas Tchérépnine
Costumes: Léon Bakst
Choreography: Michel Fokine

First produced by Sergei Diaghilev at the Théâtre de Monte Carlo, April 16, 1914

54 *Project for Decor*

Watercolor and gouache on paper, 292×464 mm. (11½×18¼ in.)
Signed, lower right, in ink (in Russian): M. Doboujinsky 1914
Exhibition: The Society of the Four Arts, 1976, No. 54

Gift of Mrs. Adolph B. Spreckels, 1959.35TD

The original decor for this production is in a private collection in Paris. Other versions are in the Lifar Collection, Wadsworth Atheneum (*Lifar,* 1965, No. 90, repr.), and the Bakhrushin Museum, Moscow.

Un Ballo in Maschera

Opera in three acts

Libretto: Antonio Somma
Music: Giuseppe Verdi

First produced at the Teatro Apollo, Rome, February 17, 1859
Produced by the Metropolitan Opera Company, New York, 1940

55 *Decor for the Audience Chamber, Act I*

Gouache on paper, 489×746 mm. (19¼×29⅜ in.)
Signed, lower right, in ink: *M Doboujinsky 1940*

Gift of Mrs. Adolph B. Spreckels, 1959.31TD

56 *Decor for the Ballroom, Act III*

Watercolor and gouache on paper, 495×749 mm. (19½×29½ in.)
Signed, lower left, in ink: *M Doboujinsky 1940*

Gift of Mrs. Adolph B. Spreckels, 1959.32TD

Ballet Imperial

Ballet in three scenes

Music: Peter Tchaikovsky
Choreography: George Balanchine

First produced by American Ballet Caravan[1] at the Hunter College Playhouse, New York, May 29, 1941

[1]. The American Ballet Caravan, founded in 1936, was the touring troupe of the American Ballet company.

57 *Decor for the Ballroom in St. Petersburg*

Pencil and watercolor on paper, 375×495 mm. (14¾×19½ in.)
Signed, lower right, in watercolor: *M Doboujinsky*
Exhibition: The Society of the Four Arts, 1976, No. 53

Gift of Mrs. Adolph B. Spreckels, 1959.33TD

Mademoiselle Angot

Ballet in one act, three scenes

Scenario: Based on Alexandre Charles Lecocq's operetta, *La Fille du Madame Angot*
Music: Alexandre Charles Lecocq
Choreography: Léonide Massine

First produced by the Ballet Theatre (today known as American Ballet Theatre), New York, October 10, 1943

58 *Decor, Act I*

Watercolor on paper, 333×444 mm. (13⅛×17½ in.)
Signed, lower right, in pencil: *M Doboujinsky / N.Y. 1946*
Exhibition: The Society of the Four Arts, 1976, No. 55

Gift of Mrs. Adolph B. Spreckels, 1959.34TD

Alexandra Exter

Belestok, near Kiev 1882 – 1949 Paris

59 *Décors de Théâtre*

    Hand-colored silkscreens on paper, 330×510 mm. (13×20 in.)

    Gift of Mr. and Mrs. Nikita D. Lobanov, 1977.25–39(P)TD (1977.30 repr.).

    This set of fifteen silkscreens was published by the Éditions des Quatres Chemins, Paris, in 1930. Many of the designs were used for musical revues in Paris in the late 1920s and early 1930s.

Michel Georges-Michel

Paris 1883 – living in Paris

60 *The Opening of "La Parade"*

    Oil on cardboard, 447×349 mm. (17⅝×13¾ in.)
    Signed, lower right, in oil: *Michel Georges-Michel / Châtelet*
    Inscribed, lower right, in oil: *Première / de Parade / Paris 1917*
    Exhibition: The Society of the Four Arts, 1976, No. 72

    Gift of Mrs. Adolph B. Spreckels, 1962.13TD

    The ballet *Parade,* with music by Eric Satie and costumes by Pablo Picasso, opened at the Théâtre du Châtelet, Paris, on May 18, 1917. Georges-Michel captured the excitement of the evening in this view of the stage from a rear box. From left to right, are: Paul Rosenberg, Marie Laurencin, Diaghilev, Misia Sert, Eric Satie, Georges-Michel, Picasso and Jean Cocteau.

Alexandre Golovine

Moscow 1863 – 1930 Pushkino

Orphée

Opera

Libretto: Jean Roger-Ducasse
Music: Jean Roger-Ducasse
Costumes: Léon Bakst

First produced at the Siloti Concerts, St. Petersburg,
  January 31, 1914
Produced by Ida Rubinstein at the Théâtre National de
  l'Opéra, Paris, June 11, 1926

61 *Decor*

Gouache on panel, 673 × 825 mm. (26½ × 32½ in.)
Signed, lower right, in ink: *A. Golovine*
Bibliography: *Bulletin of the California Palace of
  the Legion of Honor,* 1958, repr.

Gift of Mrs. Adolph B. Spreckels, 1962.30TD

Ida Rubinstein commissioned Léon Bakst to design the costumes for *Orphée* in 1924; he finished the project just before his death in December of that year. Golovine was subsequently asked to design the sets; he wrote of his work on the production, "I consider *Orphée* to be my most successful decor in opera, at least my favorite." (A. Movshenson, ed., *Alexandr Yakovlevich Golovin. Vstrechi i vpechatleniia. Pisma. Vospominaniia o Golovine,* Leningrad-Moscow, 1960, pp. 132 and 166.)

Natalia Gontcharova

Ladyzhino, near Tula 1881 – 1962 Paris

Le Coq d'Or

Opera ballet in three acts

Scenario: Vladimir Bielsky, after Alexander Pushkin, revised by Alexandre Benois
Music: Nicholas Rimsky-Korsakov
Choreography: Michel Fokine

First produced by Sergei Diaghilev at the Théâtre National de l'Opéra, Paris, May 21, 1914

62 *Project for Decor, Act I*

Pencil, watercolor and gouache on illustration board, 492 × 689 mm. (19⅜ × 27⅛ in.)
Signed, lower right, in ink: *N. Gontcharova*; below this, in pencil: *N. Gontcharova*
Inscribed, lower left, in ink: *Coq d'Or 1914 / Projet 1 tablaut* [sic]
Exhibition: The Society of the Four Arts, 1976, No. 62

Gift of Mrs. Adolph B. Spreckels, 1959.36TD

Other versions of this decor are in the collections of Evelyn Cournand, Robert Tobin, and the Bakhrushin Museum, Moscow.

63 *Costume for the Larva*

Pencil and watercolor on paper, with samples of red, yellow and blue fabric attached at left, 305 × 197 mm. (12 × 7¾ in.)
Signed, upper right, in pencil: *N. Gontcharova / 22 / N.G.*
Inscribed, upper left, in pencil: *Larve*; below this, in pencil: color notes

Gift of Mrs. Adolph B. Spreckels, 1962.51TD

The production for which Gontcharova made this costume design, dated 1922, is not known.

L'Oiseau de Feu

Ballet in one act, two scenes

Scenario: Michel Fokine
Music: Igor Stravinsky
Choreography: Michel Fokine

First produced by Sergei Diaghilev at the Théâtre National de l'Opéra, Paris, June 25, 1910 (with decors and costumes by Alexandre Golovine and Léon Bakst)
Revived by Sergei Diaghilev at the Lyceum, London, 1926

64 *Costume for the First Prince*

Pencil, watercolor and gouache on paper, 445×285 mm. (17½×11¼ in.)
Signed, upper right, in pencil: *N. Gontcharova*
Inscribed, upper left, in pencil: *l'Oiseau de Feu* /g[u]*errier*
Exhibition: The Society of the Four Arts, 1976, No. 58
Gift of Mrs. Adolph B. Spreckels, 1962.1TD

65 *Costume for a Simple Princess*

Pencil, watercolor, and silver and gold paint on paper, 452×251 mm. (17¾×9 15/16 in.)
Signed, upper left, in ink: *N. Gontcharova*
Inscribed, upper right, in pencil (in Russian): Simple Princess, 12 costumes; lower left, in pencil: *12 costumes /Princesses /Simples*; lower left, in pencil: a list of twelve dancers to use the same costume; lower right, in pencil: *N 14*; throughout, in pencil: instructions to the dressmaker

Gift of Mrs. Adolph B. Spreckels, 1962.16TD

Foire de Sorotchinsk

Opera ballet in one act

Scenario: Based on the story by Nicholas Gogol
Music: Modest Moussorgsky
Choreography: Yeltzov

Produced by the Ballets Russes de Paris at the Salle Pleyel, Paris, August, 1940

66 *Costume for a Peasant Girl*

Pencil, watercolor and gouache on paper, 476×286 mm. (18¾×11¼ in.)
Signed, lower right, in pencil: *N. Gontcharova*
Exhibition: The Society of the Four Arts, 1976, No. 57

Gift of Mrs. Adolph B. Spreckels, 1962.2TD

Chota Roustaveli

Ballet

Scenario: Nicholas Evreinoff and Serge Lifar after a fairy tale by Chota Roustaveli

Music: Selections from works by Arthur Honegger, Alexander Tchérépnine and Tibor Harsanyi

Choreography: Serge Lifar

Decors and costumes: Prince Schervachidzé and Constantin Nepokoitchitsky[1]

First produced by the Nouveau Ballet de Monte Carlo, Monte Carlo, May 5, 1946

1. Because of an argument she had with Serge Lifar, Gontcharova's designs for this ballet were never used.

67 *Project for Decor, Act I*

Pencil and watercolor on paper, 502 × 645 mm. (19¾ × 25⅜ in.)

Signed, lower left, in watercolor (over pencil): *N. Gontcharova*

Inscribed, lower right, in pencil: *I Act Barsova Chkoura / Peau de Léopard / par Chota Roustavelli* [sic]

Exhibition: The Society of the Four Arts, 1976, No. 60

Gift of Mrs. Adolph B. Spreckels, 1962.21TD

68 *Project for the Curtain*

Charcoal and watercolor on paper, 524 × 730 mm. (20⅝ × 28¾ in.)

Signed, lower left, in pencil: *N. Gontcharova*

Inscribed, lower right, in pencil: *Projet de rideau pour "Barsova Chkoura", Peau de léopard, Chota Roustavelli* [sic]

Exhibition: The Society of the Four Arts, 1976, No. 61

Gift of Mrs. Adolph B. Spreckels, 1962.20TD

69 *Costume for a Male Dancer in a Shamrock Patterned Costume*

Pencil and watercolor on paper, with samples of blue and green fabric attached across top, 308 × 220 mm. (12⅛ × 7⅞ in.)
Signed, lower right, in pencil: *N. Gontcharova*
Inscribed, upper left, in pencil: *N. 17*; upper right, in pencil: *balet* [sic] *de trefle*; lower left, in pencil: *maillot*
Exhibition: The Society of the Four Arts, 1976, No. 63

Gift of Mrs. Adolph B. Spreckels, 1962.46TD

The production for which Gontcharova designed this costume is not known. Its style and the handwriting of the inscriptions suggest that it was executed fairly late in the artist's career, probably in the 1940s.

Alexandre Jacovleff

St. Petersburg 1887 – 1938 Paris

Semiramis

Ballet

Scenario: Paul Valéry
Music: Arthur Honegger
Costumes: Alexandre Benois
Choreography: Michel Fokine

First produced by Ida Rubinstein at the Théâtre National de l'Opéra, Paris, May 11, 1934

70 *Decor, Act I*

Gouache on cardboard, 642 × 797 mm. (25¼ × 31⅜ in.)
Signed, lower right, in gouache: *A. Jacovleff*

Gift of Mrs. Adolph B. Spreckels, 1962.54TD

Another version of this decor is in the Lobanov-Rostovsky Collection (*Russian Stage and Costume Designs*, 1967, No. 76, repr.).

71 *Decor, Act II*

Gouache and gold paint on cardboard, 680×810 mm. (26¾×31⅞ in.)
Signed, lower left, in gouache: *A. Jacovleff*
Provenance: Ida Rubinstein
Exhibition: The Society of the Four Arts, 1976, No. 66
Bibliography: *Bulletin of the California Palace of the Legion of Honor,* 1958, repr.

Gift of Mrs. Adolph B. Spreckels, 1962.29TD

Alexis Korovine

Moscow 1897 – 1950 Paris

The Invisible City of Kitezh

Opera

Libretto: Vladimir Bielsky
Music: Nicholas Rimsky-Korsakov

Produced by the Opéra Privé de Maria Kousnetsov at the Théâtre des Champs-Elysées, Paris, 1929

72 *Backdrop, Act IV, Scene II*

Pen and ink and gouache on paper, 405×565 mm. (15⅞×22¼ in.)
Signed, lower right, in ink: *Alexis Korovine*
Inscribed, lower left, in ink: *Légende de la Ville Invisible de Kitège, Act IV, Tableau II*

Gift of Mr. and Mrs. Nikita D. Lobanov, 1977.10TD

Mikhail Larionov

Tiraspol, Bessarabia 1881 – 1964 Fontenay-aux-Roses, France

Soleil de Nuit

Russian scenes and dances

Music: Nicholas Rimsky-Korsakov
Choreography: Léonide Massine

First produced by Sergei Diaghilev at the Grand Théâtre, Geneva, December 20, 1915

73 *Project for the Curtain*

Pencil, watercolor and gouache on paper, 581×797 mm. (22⅞×31⅜ in.)
Signed, lower right, in watercolor: *M. Larionov* [1]*915*

Bibliography: *Bulletin of the California Palace of the Legion of Honor,* 1958, repr.

Gift of Mrs. Adolph B. Spreckels, 1962.19TD

Le Renard

Burlesque ballet with voices in one act

Scenario: Igor Stravinsky
Music: Igor Stravinsky
Choreography: Bronislava Nijinska

First produced by Sergei Diaghilev at the Théâtre National de l'Opéra, Paris, May 18, 1922

74 *Costume for the Fox as Cock*

Watercolor on paper, 486×305 mm. (19⅛×12 in.)
Signed, upper right, in watercolor: *M. Larionov*; lower left, in watercolor: *ML.* [1]*922*
Exhibition: Society of the Four Arts, 1976, No. 70

Gift of Mrs. Adolph B. Spreckels, 1962.3TD

75 *Decor with Three Figures, detail*

Watercolor on paper, 311 × 422 mm. (12¼ × 16⅝ in.)
Signed, upper left, in pencil: *M. Larionov*; lower right, in watercolor: *M.L.* [1]*921*
Exhibition: The Society of the Four Arts, 1976, No. 69

Gift of Mrs. Adolph B. Spreckels, 1962.17TD

Versions of the decor for *Le Renard* are in the Lifar Collection, Wadsworth Atheneum (*Lifar,* 1965, No. 114, repr.), the Lobanov-Rostovsky Collection and the collections of John Carr Doughty, Mme. A. Larionov, and Boris Kochno.

Marie Laurencin

Paris 1883 – 1956 Paris

Les Biches

Ballet with voices in one act

Music: Francis Poulenc
Choreography: Bronislava Nijinska

First produced by Sergei Diaghilev at the Théâtre de Monte Carlo, January 6, 1924

76 *Costume for Two Girls*

Pencil, pen and ink, and crayon on paper, 265 × 205 mm. (10 1/16 × 8 1/16 in.)
Signed, upper right, in pencil: *Marie Laurencin*
Provenance: Boris Kochno, 1958
Exhibition: The Society of the Four Arts, 1976, No. 71
Bibliography: *Bulletin of the California Palace of the Legion of Honor,* 1959, repr.; Phyllis Hattis, *Four Centuries of French Drawings in The Fine Arts Museums of San Francisco,* 1977, No. 295, repr. p. 313

Gift of Mrs. Adolph B. Spreckels, 1962.53TD

Simon Lissim

Kiev 1900 – living in Dobbs Ferry, New York

77 *Costume*

Pencil, watercolor, and silver and gold paint on paper, 310 × 197 mm. (12¼ × 7¾ in.)
Signed, center right, in ink: *S. Lissim / 23*
Bibliography: André Tessier, *Simon Lissim, étude critique,* Paris, 1928, plate 8

Gift of the artist, 1971.1TD

According to the artist this costume was executed for a fantasy Russian ballet.

La Danse Pendant le Festin

Musical Comedy
Story: Germaine Guesnier
Music: Marius-François Gaillard

Produced by the Théâtre National de l'Opéra Comique, Paris, 1931

78 *Costume*

Pencil, watercolor and gold paint on paper, 159 × 190 mm. (7½ × 6¼ in.)
Signed, lower right, in pencil: *Simon Lissim. 31*
Bibliography: Raymond Cogniat, *Simon Lissim,* Paris, 1933, plate 37

Gift of the artist, 1971.2TD

 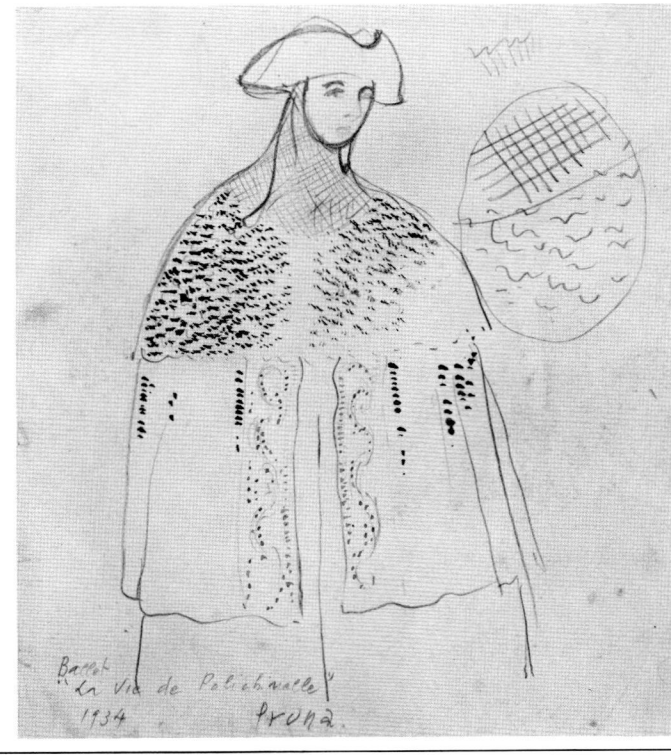

Pablo Picasso

Malaga 1881 – 1973 Mougins, France

79 *The Chinese Conjuror*

Block print on paper, 264 × 216 mm. (10⅜ × 8½ in.)
Signed, lower left, in ink: *Picasso / 1917*
Inscribed, lower left, in ink: *À Georges Michel / Souvenir de Rome / Picasso / 1917*

Gift of Mrs. Adolph B. Spreckels, 1959.50TD

Picasso based this print on his costume design for the Chinese Conjuror in *Parade,* a ballet produced by Sergei Diaghilev in 1917 (see Cat. 60). The original design is in the collection of M. Helft, *fils,* Paris.

Pedro Pruna

Barcelona 1904 – living in Barcelona

La Vie de Polichinelle

Ballet in one act, six scenes

Scenario: Claude Séran
Music: Nicholas Nabokov
Choreography: Serge Lifar

First produced by the Théâtre National de l'Opéra, Paris, June 22, 1934

80 *Costume*

Pencil and watercolor on paper, 210 × 181 mm. (8¼ × 7 1/16 in.)
Signed, lower left, in pencil: *Pruna*
Inscribed, lower left, in pencil: *Ballet / "La Vie de Polichinelle" / 1934*

Gift of Mr. and Mrs. Nikita D. Lobanov, 1977.11TD

José-Maria Sert

Barcelona 1874–1945 Barcelona

La Légende de Joseph

Ballet in one act

Scenario: Harry von Kessler and Hugo von Hofmannsthal
Music: Richard Strauss
Costumes: Léon Bakst
Choreography: Michel Fokine

First produced by Sergei Diaghilev at the Théâtre National de l'Opéra, Paris, May 17, 1914

81 *Decor*

Black and white chalk on cardboard, 686 × 768 mm. (27 × 30¼ in.)

Signed, lower right, in black chalk: *Sert / 1945*
Provenance: Boris Kochno, 1958

Gift of Mrs. Adolph B. Spreckels, 1959.39TD

Sergei Soudeikine

Smolensk 1882–1946 Nyack, New York

Petrouchka

Burlesque ballet in one act, four scenes

Scenario: Igor Stravinsky and Alexandre Benois
Music: Igor Stravinsky
Choreography: Adolph Bolm, after Michel Fokine

First produced by Sergei Diaghilev at the Théâtre du Châtelet, Paris, June 13, 1911 (with decors and costumes by Alexandre Benois)
Produced by Adolph Bolm at the Metropolitan Opera House, New York, 1925

82 *Costume for a Nobleman*

Watercolor and gouache on paper, 330×226 mm. (13×9 in.)

Signed, lower right, in ink: *Soudeikine*

Inscribed, upper left, in pencil (in another hand): *Noble;* upper right, in pencil (in another hand): *1 Ch.*[ina]*man*.

Gift of Mr. and Mrs. Nikita D. Lobanov, 1977.13TD

83 *Costume for the Mendicant Nun*

Watercolor and gouache on paper, 330×230 mm. (13×9 in.)

Signed, lower right, in ink: *Soudeikine*

Inscribed (all in another hand), upper left, in pencil: *Religieuse faisant la quête*; upper right, in pencil (in Russian): A nun; below this, in pencil: *Ballet girl/Wagner;* lower left, in pencil: *29*

Gift of Mr. and Mrs. Nikita D. Lobanov, 1977.12TD

84 *Costume for the Footman*

Watercolor and gouache on paper, 330×227 mm. (13 1/16 × 8 15/16 in.)

Signed, lower right, in ink: *Soudeikine*

Inscribed, upper left, in pencil (in another hand): *Valet de Pied/(2)*; upper right, in pencil (in another hand): *2 Ch*[ina]*man*

Gift of Mr. and Mrs. Nikita D. Lobanov, 1977.14TD

Le Rossignol

Opera in three acts

Libretto: Igor Stravinsky and Stepan Mitusov, after a fairy tale by Hans Christian Andersen
Music: Igor Stravinsky
Choreography: Boris Romanov

First produced by Alexander Sanin at the Théâtre de l'Académie Royale de Musique, Paris, May 26, 1914
Produced by the Metropolitan Opera Company, New York, March 6, 1926

85 *Costume for a Court Valet*

Pencil, gouache, and silver and gold paint on cardboard, 282 × 230 mm. (11⅛ × 9 in.)
Signed, lower right, in pencil: *Soudeikine*
Inscribed, upper right, in ink (in another hand): *36 Valet de Court (6)*
Provenance: Sotheby's, London, July 9, 1969, lot 98

Gift of Mr. and Mrs. Nikita D. Lobanov, 1977.15TD

86 *Costume for the High Priest*

Pen and ink, watercolor and gouache on paper, 275 × 220 mm. (10¾ × 8¾ in.)
Signed, lower left, in pencil: *Soudeikine*
Inscribed, upper right, in ink (in another hand): *11.Prêtre*

Gift of Mr. and Mrs. Nikita D. Lobanov, 1977.16TD

87 *Costume for the Kitchenmaid*

Pen and ink and gouache on paper, 280 × 230 mm. (11 × 9⅛ in.)
Signed, lower right, in pencil: *Soudeikine*
Inscribed, upper right, in pencil (in another hand): *3 La Cuisinière*
Provenance: Sotheby's, London, July 9, 1969, lot 97

Gift of Mr. and Mrs. Nikita D. Lobanov, 1977.17TD

88 *Costume for a Page*

Pencil, gouache, and silver and gold paint on paper, 281 × 230 mm. (11 1/16 × 9 in.)
Signed, lower right, in pencil: *Soudeikine*
Inscribed, upper right, in ink (in another hand): *35 Pages*
Provenance: Sotheby's, London, July 9, 1969, lot 99

Gift of Mr. and Mrs. Nikita D. Lobanov, 1977.18TD

Pen and ink and gouache on paper, 277 × 230 mm. (11 × 9 1/16 in.)
Signed, lower right, in pencil: *Soudeikine*
Inscribed, upper right, in pencil (in another hand): *18 Pages Femmes (4)*
Provenance: Sotheby's, London, July 9, 1969, lot 100

Gift of Mr. and Mrs. Nikita D. Lobanov, 1977.19TD

Sergei Tchehonine

Novgorod 1878 – 1936 Paris

The Snow Maiden

Ballet

Scenario: Sergei Denham
Music: Alexander Glazunov
Choreography: Bronislava Nijinska

Project, Ballets Russes de Vera Nemtchinova, Paris, 1931

90 *Costume for a Snow Maiden*

Pencil, pen and ink, and watercolor on paper, 182 × 90 mm. (7 × 3½ in.)
Signed, lower left, in ink: *S. Tchehonine*

Gift of Mr. and Mrs. Nikita D. Lobanov, 1977.20TD

91 *Costume for a Maid*

Pencil, pen and ink, and watercolor on paper, 316 × 230 mm. (12½ × 9 1/16 in.)
Signed, lower right, in pencil: *S. Tchehonine/Paris*

Gift of Mr. and Mrs. Nikita D. Lobanov, 1977.21TD

From 1928 until his death, Tchehonine lived in Paris. There he designed musical revues for the Opéra Privé de Madame Kousnetsov. This costume was probably for one of them, although the exact production is not known.

Pavel Tchelitchew

Moscow 1898 – 1957 Rome

92 *Decor*

Gouache and silver paint on paper, 190 × 290 mm. (7½ × 11⅜ in.)

Signed, on verso, in ink: *P. Tchelitchew*

Provenance: Schoura Zaoussailoff (sister of the artist); Richard Nathanson, 1976

Bibliography: Richard Nathanson, *Pavel Tchelitchew, a Collection of 54 Theater Designs,* catalogue to an exhibition held at the Alpine Club, London, December 13 – 22, 1976, p. 12

Gift of Mr. and Mrs. Nikita D. Lobanov, 1977.22TD

This design and *Costume for a Priest* (Cat. 93) were probably executed by Tchelitchew in Istanbul and Sofia between 1919 and 1921. During those years he worked on a number of productions for Boris Kniasseff and the Victor P. Zimin Ballet Company.

93 *Costume for a Priest*

Watercolor and gouache on paper, 300 × 195 mm. (11 15/16 × 7¾ in.)

Signed, on verso, in ink: *P. Tchelitchew*

Provenance: Schoura Zaoussailoff (sister of the artist); Richard Nathanson, 1976

Bibliography: Richard Nathanson, *Pavel Tchelitchew, a Collection of 54 Theatre Designs,* catalogue to an exhibition held at the Alpine Club, London, December 13 – 22, 1976, p. 11

Gift of Mr. and Mrs. Nikita D. Lobanov, 1977.23TD

Bibliography

The bibliography is divided into five sections. In the last section, the artists are listed according to the westernized spelling of their names used in this catalogue. However, in view of the diversity of spellings encountered (for example, Alexandre Benois, Alexandr Benua, Alexander Benois), the transliterated Russian names plus patronymics together with the main variants are included in parentheses.

In most cases reference is made *only* to important and/or recent publications. Where appropriate, these titles are intended to supplement the sources listed on pages 98 through 105 of the catalogue of the exhibition *Russian Painters and the Stage 1884–1965* (see Frequently Cited References). Further bibliographical information will be found in the standard reference manuals, especially in the catalogue of dance holdings of The New York Public Library, entitled *Dictionary Catalog of the Dance Collection* (Boston: Hall, 1974) and its supplementary volumes, *Bibliographical Guide to Dance* (1975 through 1978).

Reference Manuals

1. New York Public Library, *Dictionary Catalog of the Dance Collection* (Boston: Hall, 1974), in 10 vols. Regular supplements issued.
2. T. Gorina *et al.* (eds.), *Khudozhniki narodov SSSR. Biobibliograficheskii slovar* (Moscow: Iskusstvo, 1976), Vol. 3.

Books on Modern Russian Art and the Stage

1. E. Rakitina, *V zerkale stseny* (Moscow: Znanie, 1975).
2. Georges Wakhevitch, *L'Envers des Décors* (Paris: Laffont, 1977).
3. Janet Kennedy, *The Mir iskusstva Group and Russian Art 1898–1912* (New York: Garland, 1977).
4. Alla Mikhailova, *Obraz spektaklia* (Moscow: Iskusstvo, 1978).
5. F. Syrkina and E. Kostina, *Russkoe teatralno-dekoratsionnoe iskusstvo* (Moscow: Iskusstvo, 1978).
6. M. Guerman, *Art of the October Revolution* (New York: Abrams, 1979).
7. John E. Bowlt, *The Silver Age: Russian Art of the Early Twentieth Century and the "World of Art" Group* (Newtonville: ORP, 1979).
8. E. Rakitina, *Khudozhnik, stsena. Shornik statei* (Moscow: Sovetskii Khudozhnik, 1978).

Catalogues of Exhibitions Relating to Stage Sets and Costumes by Modern Russian and Other Artists

1. *Omaggio ai disegnatori di Diaghilev* (Venice: Palazzo Grassi, 1975).
2. *Vsevolod Emilievich Meierkhold. Yubileinaia vystavka k stoletiiu so dnia rozhdeniia 1874–1974* (Moscow: Nauka, 1976).
3. *Khudozhniki Bolshogo teatra za 200 let* (Moscow: Iskusstvo, 1976).
4. *Diaghilev i balletti russi e il loro tempo* (Rome: Libreria i Galleria Pan, 1977).
5. *Diaghilev's Ballets Russes 1909–1929* (Cambridge, Mass.: Harvard University, 1977).
6. *Mastera sovetskoi stsenografii* (Moscow: Novosti, 1977).
7. *Russkoe teatralno-dekoratsionnoe iskusstvo iz sobranii I.V. Kachurina i Ya.E. Rubinshteina* (Tallin: State Art Museum of Estonia, 1978).
8. *Mikhail Larionov: Designs for the Ballet "The Adventures of Karaguez"* (Syracuse: Everson Museum of Art, 1978).
9. *Designs for the New York Stage* (Westchester: Pace University, 1978).
10. *Diaghilev: Costumes and Designs of the Ballets Russes* (New York: The Metropolitan Museum of Art, 1978).
11. *Diaghilev et les Ballets Russes* (Paris: La Bibliothèque Nationale, 1979).
12. *Dance Image: A Tribute to Serge Diaghilev* (Jackson, Miss.: Museum of Art, 1979).

Auction Catalogues Relating to Stage Sets, Costumes and Other Works by Modern Russian and Other Artists

1. *The Diaghilev-Lifar Library,* Sotheby Parke Bernet, Monte Carlo, 1975.
2. *Important 19th and 20th Century Drawings and Watercolors Collected by the Late Lester Avnet,* Sotheby Parke Bernet, New York, 1976.
3. *Ballet and Theatre Material,* Sotheby & Co., London, 1977.
4. *Ballet and Theatre Material,* Sotheby & Co., London, 1978.
5. *Russian and European Avant-Garde Art: 1905–1930,* Sotheby Parke Bernet, New York, 1978.
6. *Dance. Theatre. Opera. Costume and Decor Designs. Drawings. Prints and Books,* Sotheby Parke Bernet, New York, 1978.
7. *Ballet and Theatre Material,* Sotheby & Co., London, 1979.
8. *Russian and European Avant-Garde Art: 1905–1930,* Sotheby Parke Bernet, New York, 1979.

Publications Relating to Individual Artists

Anisfeldt, Boris (Anisfeld, Boris, or Ber Izrailevich)

1. *Boris Anisfeld,* exhibition catalogue (New York: Brooklyn Museum, 1918). Circulated 1918–20.
2. *Boris Anisfeld,* exhibition catalogue (Chicago: The Art Institute, 1958).
3. O. Voltsenburg et al. (eds.), *Khudozhniki narodov SSSR. Biobibliograficheskii slovar* (Moscow: Iskusstvo, 1970), Vol. 1, p. 159
4. *Boris Anisfeldt: 20 Years of Design for the Theater,* exhibition catalogue (Washington, D.C.: Smithsonian Institution, 1971).
5. *Boris Anisfeld 1879–1973,* exhibition catalogue, The William Benton Museum of Art (University of Connecticut: Storrs, 1979).

Bakst, Léon (Bakst, Lev Samoilovich)

1. C. Spencer, *Léon Bakst* (London: Academy Editions, 1973).
2. I. Pruzhan, *Bakst* (Leningrad: Iskusstvo, 1975).
3. L. Senelich and David Brownell, *The Sleeping Beauty Ballet. Léon Bakst's Design for the Music of Tchaikovsky* (San Francisco: Ballerophan Books, 1977).

Benois, Alexandre (Benua, Alexandr Nikolaevich, or Benois, Alexander)

1. M. Etkind, *Alexandr Nikolaevich Benua* (Leningrad–Moscow: Iskusstvo, 1965).
2. *Alexandre Benois. Il classico della rivoluzione 1870–1970,* exhibition catalogue (Milan: La Scala, 1970–71).
3. Yu. Gogolitsyn, "Benua v Russkom muzee," in *Stroitelnyi rabochii,* 1974, No. 28, p. 10.
4. E. Klimov, "Vstrechi," in *Novoe russkoe slovo,* July 16, 1978, p. 4.

Berman, Eugène (Berman, Evgenii Gustavovich)

1. *Eugène Berman,* exhibition catalogue (Boston: The Institute of Modern Art, 1941–42).
2. *Eugène Berman,* exhibition catalogue (Buenos Aires: Instituto de arte moderno, 1950).
3. "Eugène Berman," obituary in *The New York Times,* December 15, 1972, p. 52.

Bilinsky, Boris Konstantinovich

1. A.P.V., "B. K. Bilinsky," in *Teatr i iskusstvo,* 1924, No. 2, p. 10.
2. *Boris Bilinsky,* exhibition catalogue (New York: Leonard Hutton Galleries, 1975).

Bouchène, Dmitri (Bushen, Dmitrii Dmitrievich)

1. S. Ivensky, *Mastera russkogo exlibrisa* (Leningrad: Khudozhnik RSFSR, 1973), pp. 102–05.
2. V. Veidle, "Posledniaia kniga serebrianogo veka," in *Russkaia mysl,* December 8, 1978, p. 9.

Doboujinsky, Mstislav (Dobujinsky or Dobuzhinsky, Mstislav Valerianovich)

1. I. Korsakate, *Mstislavas Dobužinskis* (Vilnius: Vaga, 1975).
2. *Mstislav V. Dobujinsky. A Centenary Exhibition,* exhibition catalogue (Oxford: The Ashmolean Museum, 1975).
3. M. Dobuzhinsky, "O risunkakh Pushkina," in *Novyi zhurnal,* 1976, No. 125.
4. M. Dobuzhinsky, "Iz pisem i dnevnikov," in *Tvorchestvo,* 1976, No. 11, pp. 12–15.
5. A. Lupandina, "Dobuzhinsky v teatre," in *Sovetskie khudozhniki teatra i kino '75* (Moscow: Sovetskii khudozhnik, 1977), pp. 189–92.
6. E. Klimov, "Vstrechi," in *Novoe russkoe slovo,* September 15, 1978, p. 2.
7. *Mstislav V. Dobujinsky: Half a Century of Theatrical Art 1907–1957,* exhibition catalogue (New York: Lincoln Center, 1978).

Exter, Alexandra (Exter, Alexandra Alexandrovna)

1. A. Nakov, *Alexandra Exter* (Paris: Galerie Chauvelin, 1972).
2. *Artist of the Theater. Alexandra Exter,* exhibition catalogue (New York: Lincoln Center, 1974).
3. *Alexandra Exter. Marionettes,* exhibition catalogue (New York: Leonard Hutton Galleries, 1975).
4. V. Rakitin, "Marsiane A. Exter," in *Dekorativnoe iskusstvo,* 1977, No. 4, pp. 29–30.

Georges-Michel, George

Nothing substantial has been published on Georges-Michel.

Golovine, Alexandre (Golovin, Alexandr Yakovlevich)

1. A. Movshenson (ed.), *Alexandr Yakovlevich Golovin. Vstrechi i vpechatleniia. Pisma. Vospominaniia o Golovine* (Leningrad–Moscow: Iskusstvo, 1960).
2. A. Bassekhes, *Teatr i zhivopis Golovina* (Moscow: Izobrazitelnoe iskusstvo, 1970).
3. S. Onufrieva, *Golovin* (Leningrad: Iskusstvo, 1977).

Gontcharova, Natalia (Goncharova, Natalia Sergeevna)

1. M. Chamot, *Gontcharova* (Paris: La Bibliothèque des Arts, 1972).
2. *Larionov–Gontcharova Rétrospective,* exhibition catalogue (Brussels: Musée d'Ixelles, 1976).
3. T. Logina, "Larionov i Goncharova v sovremennom iskusstve," in *Russkaia mysl,* August 2, 1979, p. 10, and August 9, p. 8.

Jacovleff, Alexandre (Yakovlev or Iacovleff, Alexandr Evgenievich)

1. *Alexandre Iacovleff (1887–1938),* exhibition catalogue (Cambridge, Mass.: Gropper Art Gallery, 1972).
2. E. Klimov, "Alexandr Yakovlev," in *Novoe ruskoe slovo,* June 24, 1973, p. 5.

Korovine, Alexis (Korovin, Alexei Konstantinovich)

Nothing substantial has been published on Alexis Korovine. The reader will find scattered references to him in:

1. N. Moleva, *Konstantin Korovin. Zhizn i tvorchestvo* (Moscow: Akademiia khudozhestv SSSR, 1963).
2. I. Zilbershtein and V. Samkov (eds.), *Konstantin Korovin vspominaet...* (Moscow: Izobrazitelnoe iskusstvo, 1971).

Larionov, Mikhail (Larionov, Mikhail Fedorovich)

1. *Larionov – Gontcharova Rétrospective,* exhibition catalogue (Brussels: Musée d'Ixelles, 1976).
2. B. Kokhno, "Mikhail Larionov — khudozhnik-khoreograf," in *Russkaia mysl,* December 8, 1977, p. 11.
3. Michel Larionov, *Une Avant-Garde Explosive* (Lausanne: L'Age d'homme, 1978).
4. G. Pospelov, "O 'valetakh' bubnovykh i valetakh chervonnykh," in *Panorama iskusstv 77* (Moscow: Sovetskii khudozhnik, 1978), pp. 127–143.
5. M. Daulte, "Larionov et l'Art Néo-primitif russe," in *L'Oeil,* June, 1979, pp. 44–51.
6. T. Logina, "Larionov i Goncharova v sovremennom iskusstve," in *Russkaia mysl,* August 2, 1979, p. 10, and August 9, p. 8.

Laurencin, Marie

1. J. Cocteau, *La difficulté d'être* (Monte Carlo: Rocher, 1953).
2. Charlotte Gere, *Marie Laurencin* (New York: Rizzoli, 1977).

Lissim, Simon (Lisim, Semen Mikhailovich)

1. R. Cogniat, G. Lechavallier-Chevignard and Louis Réau, *Simon Lissim* (Paris: Editions du Cygne, 1933).
2. *Dreams in the Theatre. Designs of Simon Lissim,* exhibition catalogue. Exhibition originated at Lincoln Center, New York. Circulated 1975–76.
3. *The World of Simon Lissim. 90 Designs for the Theatre,* exhibition catalogue. Circulated by the International Exhibitions Foundation, Washington, D.C., 1979.

Picasso, Pablo

Douglas Cooper, *Picasso Theatre* (New York: Abrams, 1968).

Pruna, Pedro

Sebastian Gasch and Pedro Pruna, *De la danza* (Barcelona: Barna, 1946).

Sert, José-Maria

Nothing substantial has been published on José-Maria Sert. General references will be found in:
1. Misia Sert, *Misia* (Paris: Gallimard, 1952).
2. J. Cocteau, "Preface," in *Misia and the Muses: the Memoirs of Misia Sert* (New York: Day, 1953).

Soudeikine, Sergei (Sudeikine, Sergei Yurievich)

D. Kogan, *Sergei Sudeikin* (Moscow: Iskusstvo, 1974).

Tchehonine, Sergei (Chekhonin, Sergei Vasilievich)

1. A. Efros and N. Punin, *S. Chekhonin* (Moscow–Petrograd: Gosudarstvennoe izdatelstvo, 1923). Editions in Russian, English and French.
2. Yu. Gerchuk, "Iskusstvo Sergeia Chekhonina," in *Tvorchestvo,* 1978, No. 2, pp. 20–23.
3. Natalia Lianda, "Sergei Chkhonin and the New Soviet Porcelain," in *Soviet Union* (Tempe: Arizona State University, forthcoming), Vol. 7, Parts 1 and 2.

Tchelitchew, Pavel (Chelichev or Tschelischtscheff, Pavel Fedorovich)

1. P. Tyler, *The Divine Comedy of Pavel Tchelitchew* (London: Weidenfeld and Nicolson, 1967).
2. *Pavel Tchelitchew (1898–1957): A Collection of Fifty-Four Theatre Designs c. 1919–1923,* exhibition catalogue (London: The Alpine Club, 1976).
3. Alexandr Bakhrakh, "Monparnasskie vstrechi," in *Novoe russkoe slovo,* September 2, 1979, pp. 5, 7.